How Do I Go Forward Without You?

By Narseary Williams Harris

Copyright © 2013 by Narseary Williams Harris
Printed in USA by Greater Is He Publishing

Author: Narseary Williams Harris
Editor: Shann Hall-LochmannVanBennekom
Jacket Designer: Rob King
Layout: Ileta Randall

Grateful acknowledgement is made for permission to reprint "Sickle Cell Disease" by Kevin Pompei, Associate Director of Genetic Science at the University of Utah. All rights reserved. Used by permission.

ISBN 978-1-938950-20-9

Greater is He Publishing Company
9824 E. Washington St. Chagrin Falls Ohio 44023
P O. Box 46115 Bedford Ohio, 44146

http://www.greaterishepublishing.com

Dedication

This book is dedicated to the memory of my two sons, Paul King David and King Solomon.

To my husband Vernal, thank you for your love and support while I wrote this book. Thank you for your prayers and encouragement. I sometimes (well, a lot of the time) wrote through breakfast, lunch, and dinner, so we had to go out to eat. Narseary's kitchen is now open.

To my son Elijah, whom I love dearly, and am so very proud of.

To my granddaughter Malaya and my grandson Solomon Jr.

To my extraordinary supportive family and friends.

To Bishop Dr. Carolyn Boston Love, who obeyed the leading of the Holy Spirit to Prophecy into my life, allowing me to write this book.

I truly thank God for placing you all in my life.

You all have been a part of this journey, bringing life to the pages of my book.

To God be the Glory!

Introduction

For many years I have urged Mrs. Narseary Harris to present to the world, in writing, this awesome testimony that was down in her spirit.

I have known the Harris Family for nearly 35 years. They are a tight knit and loving family. Pastor Vernal Harris and Lady Narseary Harris raised their multi-gifted sons in the fear and admonition of the Lord.

One might think that with having accepted your call to ministry and doing all that you possibly can do to bring glory to the kingdom of God, that that your life should flow reassuringly well. Such was not the case with the Harris's. Two of their three wonderful sons died of that dreaded disease called Sickle Cell Anemia.

I, along with countless others throughout the community, watched in utter awe as this brave couple stood as shining example of the faithfulness of Jesus Christ in the face of horrendous tragedy.

In her book entitled "HOW DO I GO FORWARD WITHOUT YOU?" Narseary details, in gripping transparency, her journey through living with and having to let go of the sons that she loved so dearly.

I applaud the Harris's for their willingness and bravery in sharing with the world this story of Hurt, Healing, and Hope.

Bishop Jeffery Melvin
Presiding Prelate
Rwanda East Africa Jurisdiction
Church of God in Christ

Foreword

I have been privileged to know the Rev. Vernal Harris and his devoted and activist wife Narseary, for more than 25 years, during their ministry in Rochester and Buffalo NY. They are both inspiring people, in their parish ministry and in their community service. Believing that the Christian ministry should not be confined behind four walls, they have engaged in committed parental engagement with their sons' education and in community revitalization efforts in the neighborhoods where they resided. Their musically talented sons have made them proud, as well as inspiring those under the sound of their voices and batons with the music they composed and directed.

Despite all of these positive services, these parents have witnessed adversity as few have. Their two oldest sons, Paul and Solomon, succumbed to Sickle Cell Anemia at the tender ages of 26 and 33 respectively. In the past 13 years, their faith was tested beyond comprehension. Yet they and their youngest son, Elijah, have come through unbelievable pain and heartache to serve even stronger than before. Narseary Harris has chronicled these devastating events into a story of perseverance, tenacity, and unshakable faith. There is no greater trauma for parents than the loss of a child, and the loss of two children is incalculable. Yet this family has survived, been strengthened and continued to serve.

In these pessimistic times, the examples of Narseary and Vernal Harris motivate us to do more than just "hang in there", but to serve our communities and our congregations with renewed strength. They are my friends and role models.

William A. Johnson, Jr.
Mayor of Rochester, 1994-2005
April 2013

Table of Contents

CHAPTER ONE

God Is So Awesome

Dear God, I really do not understand why you had to take my sons. So many people told us that the boys would be healed from Sickle Cell Anemia. They said my boys were going to have a testimony out of this world. They said Paul was going to tell of how you healed him miraculously, and that people everywhere would give you the honor and the glory. I don't know what happened. Were all those people wrong? Were they just saying what they thought I wanted to hear? Was I reading something more into their words that wasn't really there? I just don't understand. What happened, Lord? What happened? I even told my children that you were going to heal them. I told them we just needed to do our part by praying, by believing your word, and to keep speaking healing as though it were already done. Was I wrong too? I've been told ever since I was a child that I should not question you, but I just don't understand this.

There are some things in life that we may never understand, and I mean NEVER!

At times, I had thought my experiences might make me lose my mind or even kill me. Many times, I found myself wanting to give up and throw in the towel, but unbeknownst to me, God had a plan.

At age eleven, I gave my heart to the Lord. God opened my eyes to His awesome power when He had healed my mother of an illness that she had suffered from for as long as I could remember.

Mommy had gone to a little store-front church in the neighborhood. When she came home after church, she seemed different somehow. One night I realized that she was eating an apple. I noticed it because she had had difficulty eating and drinking anything—let alone an apple! There was a sense of new peace about her. She seemed to be joyful and pain free. Days later, after that first church visit, I ascertained that she wasn't smoking cigarettes or drinking alcohol anymore.

The next time she went to church, I requested to go with her. The people sang, shouted, and danced. Someone asked me if I wanted to be saved and I said yes. The saints prayed for, and with me, until I received the Holy Ghost! I can't say I really understood all that had happened that night, but I am glad that it happened.

At a young age, God called me to serve in the ministry. All of the details weren't clear, but I knew that I loved God and I needed to pray. I wanted to go to church and loved the worship services. Even at home or in school, I felt the desire in my heart to pray.

When I was twelve-years-old, God gave me the gifts of prophecy; laying on hand to heal the sick; and made me a prayer warrior. I had seen with my own eyes, the miraculous healing power of God. I witnessed blinded eyes made to see.

People in our community had heard how God would heal people by the laying on of hands and through the prayers of my mother. I remember one time when my mommy was asked to go to pray for a woman in our community who was totally blind in both eyes. The lady believed that if Sister Ruth (my mom) would come to her home and pray for her that she would see again.

Needless to say, that is exactly what happened. Mommy entered the woman's house and asked, "Do you believe if I lay my hands on you and we pray for you to see, that God will heal you?"

"Oh yes, I believe, Sister Ruth!"

Mommy laid her hands on the lady. "God, in the name of Jesus, please restore this woman's sight. Amen." Mommy stood up. "Can you see?"

The lady grasped Mommy's hands. "Oh my, yes. Yes, I can see!"

Everyone in the room waved their hands and praised God. Mommy turned her to the window. "Tell me what you see."

The lady said, "It's blurry, but I can see light and shapes."

Mommy told her, "Your sight is going to become clearer each day.'"

I was reminded of the passage in Mark 8:22-25, where Jesus healed the blind man and asked him what he saw. The man told Jesus that he saw men as trees. Later the man was able to see all things normally.

A few days later, the woman's housekeeper called my mom and said, "She was sitting in a chair in front of the living room window. Then she turned to me and announced that she could see the colors of each car driving by. She could see every color: red, blue, white. Oh how amazing! Glory be to God!"

When I was in high school, we had to take swimming lessons. I was not good at it and I have not yet learned to swim. I would come up with different excuses to avoid that pool. One day at gym class, I told the Physical Education teacher that my foot was sore and hurting, and that it felt like there were two bumps on the bottom of it.

"Let me have a look," she asked. When she looked at my foot a funny expression came over her face. She said, "I think you need to go the school nurse's office."

The nurse took one look at my foot and said, "You cannot go back to gym class without a note from the doctor saying the warts had been treated or removed." I was very happy to hear that. YAY! No more swim class for me.

After getting home from school that day, I told my mom what the nurse said and she asked to see my foot. Without any hesitation, she prayed for me. I took my bath that night and while drying off, I noticed two small holes in the bottom of my foot. The two warts had fallen out in the bathtub. I quickly placed my hand over the drain to catch them before they disappeared. I yelled out, "Mommy, come and see this!" I was still looking at my foot and showed her where the two small holes now were.

No surgery, no freezing meds, I just experienced the power of healing, through believing in the power of prayer, and faith that God would heal me. God still works miracles. These are just a few testimonies that I witnessed at different times in my youth. There are so many, many more that I could share. I saw God deliver people from demon possession. I know God can heal. There is no doubt in my mind of that truth.

So, I guess I thought that because of this, I would be able to handle the troubles that I would encounter on my journey. I found out that it would help, but it did not take the problems away. This walk proved to be a totally different experience than I had ever imagined. I learned the worth and value of fasting and praying. I learned the benefits of reading and studying God's word. I learned to have faith and to put my trust in God, even when I did not see a way out. So why did my life take such drastic turns of events?

A young preacher came to the church that my family attended. I was only sixteen at the time and had no idea that this man would become my future husband. Since I was only seventeen when I married this gentle man, my dad had to sign a form granting us permission. I graduated from high school on Friday and was married the next day. This is where my journey begins.

Chapter Two

An Answered Prayer

We'd been married for five years, but still had no children. I'd been fasting and praying while asking God to bless me with a child. I was so sad. I felt inadequate as a wife and unfulfilled as a woman. Before we were married, my husband had a daughter from a previous relationship, so he knew what fatherhood was like and didn't seem to mind that we hadn't had a child together yet. He would tell me not to worry and that when the time was right we'd have our baby. I felt that he really didn't understand. I kept asking my doctor what was wrong with me, and he agreed with my husband, that in time I'd get pregnant. My doctor put me on hormone pills. That didn't work. I was taking my temperature every day trying to be sure I didn't miss my ovulation. Finally, after three years, I became pregnant. Boy, oh boy! I was so happy. My family and friends were so excited for me. We were hoping for a little boy because my husband already had a little girl.

One evening, I started to have what I thought was a bad tummy ache. I was only six months pregnant, so being in labor was the farthest thing from my mind. Sure enough that was exactly what was happening. I was having premature labor and would have my baby that same night.

I could not believe after waiting so long to get pregnant that I would deliver a stillborn child. I was going to have a baby girl. She was so tiny and precious. I wanted to hold her and tell her how happy I was when I found out she was coming into my life, and now how sorry I was that she and I were not going to have that mother-daughter relationship I'd been waiting for, for so long. I cried so hard that I don't even remember when I finally stopped. My husband was away at church when I went into labor that night, so my friend, Sissy, took me to the hospital. I will always remember and thank her for being there for me at such a pivotal time in my life.

Because my husband was not there, I felt so alone in that labor room even though the doctor and nurse were with me. My mom had come to the hospital my now. But where was God? Did He see what was going on in that room? Where was my husband? He was a preacher, a man of God. Why did I have to go through this alone? Did I do something wrong? Was I out of the will of God? Was my desire to be a mother not His plan for me? Had I been asking for something that was not meant for me? Was I being punished for something that I'd done wrong in my life, and if so, what? *Lord Jesus, help me please!*

If that was not bad enough, I still went through all the emotions of having a newborn child. I had planned to breastfeed, and although my baby girl didn't survive after the delivery, I still produced milk. That was hard to bear because it reminded me that my child did not live.

I became pregnant again about six months later. I lost that baby about two months in. The doctor was not able to tell the gender of the baby. He asked if I had fallen or something because the fetus was torn apart. I had not fallen, though. All I know is that I had started bleeding and it wouldn't stop. *What went wrong this time? My dear Lord! Not again. I lost two children! WHY? Why was this happening to me?* I was beginning to think it was not

God's will for me to have children. Yet, I still wanted to be a mother and was not willing to give up yet. Surely, there had to be a logical reason why I couldn't carry a child to term.

I related to Hannah in the Bible when she went to the temple to pray. (I Samuel 1:10-19) The priest saw her moving her mouth and thought she was drunken. I even told the Lord, that if He would let me have a child, then I would give the child back to Him.

I finally got pregnant and gave birth to our first son, Paul King David Harris. His dad named him Paul King David after two of his favorite men in the bible. At that time, I wasn't sure if I really liked the name. I wanted to name him Vernal Lee Harris, the third, after his dad. As he grew into the young man that he did, I realized that his life reflected the lives of the same Biblical men for whom he was named.

God finally answered my prayer.

At birth, Paul didn't cry right away. I waited and longed to hear that little baby cry. I was terrified that the doctor was going to tell me my baby did not survive delivery, like my little girl before him. I never heard her cry.

I asked my doctor, "Why isn't my baby crying? Is he okay?"

He said, "Don't worry, he's okay." Then he tapped him on the bottom of his tiny little feet and I heard it! That cry that let me know he was alive! I finally had my baby. A beautiful baby boy! Oh, the joy that I felt. I cannot even begin to explain the happiness I felt at that moment. He was perfect, just perfect. Yep, I counted to be sure he had all ten toes and all ten fingers. He was just the cutest little thing. I put him to my breast and he began to nurse. I felt like a real mom for the first time. I loved that little boy so much. All was well with my world. The wait had been so worth it.

I remember, after I came home with Paul from the hospital, I was a bit nervous about giving him his first bath. Thank God, Mommy lived next door and gladly came over to help me give him his bath. Well, the truth is she bathed him while I watched. I did it the next time by myself though.

After Paul was about six months old, my husband moved us to New London, Connecticut. I wasn't too keen on the idea. I didn't know anyone there. Paul was my first child and Mommy's first grandchild, so I had been depending on her to help me with this new phase of my life called motherhood. I was not at all happy about moving away from home, but we moved anyway.

My Paul was so fat and cute. He had rolls on his thighs and arms. He had fat cheeks that we could not resist kissing and pinching, plus an adorable double chin. He was a bouncing baby boy with a jovial laugh. He was a happy baby.

I noticed that he was not crawling when we'd put him down on the floor to play. He seemed to have trouble bending his knees. He didn't crawl before he walked, but by the time he was nine months old, he was walking on his own. He finally learned to crawl after we had our second son, King Solomon D. Harris. Paul saw his brother creeping on the floor and decided to follow after his little brother. Too cute!

Shortly after we had moved to Connecticut, my mom

came to visit. Paul was her first grandchild, so she was a very proud grandma. She had planned to take a trip to Detroit to visit family and asked if she could take Paul along. She wanted to show off her new grandson. She was going on the train and that was going to be his first train ride and the first time he would be away from me for any longer than a few hours. I had mixed feelings about it, but we finally decided to let him go. She was only going for a few days and I would drive to her house in Rochester, New York to pick him up when they returned. I called her every day to check on him.

Mommy later told me that while they were on the trip, Paul was very fussy. I think at first Mommy thought he was just missing me. She also noticed, though, that when she changed his diapers, the urine looked quite dark.

When she picked him up, he cried. He didn't seem to want to be held or touched. Mom told me that he cried when my cousins would try to pick him up to play with him. After a few days, he seemed to be better.

Vernal and I drove to Rochester to pick Paul up. My heart sunk when we arrived at Mommy's house because when I reached for Paul, he didn't reach back for me. I thought he was upset with me because he hadn't seen me for a while. I took him in my arms and hugged and kissed him. He laid his little head on my shoulder. I cooed in his ear. "Oh my darling little boy, Mommy is so sorry for being away from you. I love you and missed you so much." I hugged and kissed him some more, and finally, he smiled. He didn't want to be out of my sight. Boy, did I feel guilty for a while that I let him go to Detroit without me.

After we got back to Connecticut, things seemed to get back to normal. One day my husband and I had a babysitter come over to sit with Paul so we could go out for a while. We had made friends with a couple we'd met who lived in our neighborhood. They had a little girl who was just a little older, so we thought Paul would have fun playing with her.

When we got back home, Paul was sitting on the sofa with dried tear trails that had run down his cheeks. He had such a sad look on his face. A look that reminded me of the time we went to pick him up from Mommy. I thought, *Oh no. I made my baby boy sad again.* I felt like a bad mother. I went over to pick him up from the sofa and he began to cry, and I mean really cry. I asked our friend, "Why is he just sitting here and not playing?"

She said, "I don't know. He has been screaming the whole time you were gone. I couldn't do anything to appease him so I just let him sit there and cry. I think he's just spoiled and only is happy if his Momma is nearby."

Later, after I'd begun to get Paul ready for bed, I noticed that his arms and legs were swollen and red. His little fingers were so puffy that they reminded me of how a rubber glove looks when it's blown up like a balloon. There wasn't any space between his little fingers. I thought, "What in the world is this?" I had not seen him like that before then. I mean, he did have chubby hands, but not like that.

I asked, "What happened to his arms and legs?"

She answered, "I don't know. I didn't even notice it."

Then I began to worry. "Did he fall or did you drop him?"

My friend bristled. "I can't believe you would think that I would do such a thing. I thought we were friends."

I knew she felt bad, but so did I, however, my bigger concern focused on Paul. After she left with her daughter, I started to get Paul ready for bed, but he became even fussier and his cries turned into screams. No matter what I tried, rocking, singing, rubbing his back, he would not be comforted. This was not the norm for him; he usually loved cuddling with me after his bath.

Then I noticed that his knees and elbows felt warm to the touch, and it seemed to pain him if I touched his joints. He stiffened his body and tried to jerk away when I touched his knees and elbows. I could tell even my gentle touch hurt him. I rushed to find my husband. "I think we should take Paul to the hospital."

After the doctor examined Paul, he asked, "Did either one of you drop him?"

In shock and feeling crushed that they believed I could hurt my precious baby, I answered, "No, of course not!"

When I realized they didn't believe me, my mind rushed back to how I had accused my babysitter of the same thing. I yearned to tell her how sorry I was to think that she could have done anything to hurt him.

The doctor glared at me while tapping his foot. "Are you sure you didn't drop him?"

Swallowing back tears, I covered my face with my hands. "I'm positive. He was fine when we left, the babysitter insisted that he didn't fall and I believe her. As soon as I noticed his arms and legs, we rushed him to the hospital."

I could feel the medical staff judging me. How could any mother hurt a precious child? My mother's intuition told me that Baby Paul was seriously sick. Why didn't the doctors do something instead of point their fingers at my husband and me?

Finally, they took him in for x-rays of his little arms and legs. They believed they may have been broken, but the results all came back normal. They, then, told us that they were going to draw blood to run some more tests.

One of the doctors asked me, "Do you know if you have the sickle trait?"

My OB/GYN doctor had told me that I carried the trait, but when I questioned him about it, he reassured me that I only needed to worry if my husband also carried the trait too. I asked him if my husband should have a blood test or something to see if he did have the trait, but he insisted that it wasn't necessary. I really didn't think any more of it. I wished I'd insisted that he had my husband come in to be tested, too.

The ER doctor asked my husband, "Do you know if you carry the trait?"

He shook his head. "I don't think so."

The doctor said, "Well, Mr. Harris, we believe this child has Sickle Cell Anemia and that can happen only if both parents have the trait."

He told the doctor again that he did not think he had the trait, but the doctor thought it best to draw some blood and check for sure. It was an important step in diagnosing Paul. My husband is soooooo afraid of needles, but he gave them his arm. Big baby! Afterward, he left the room where Paul and I sat waiting for the test results. When he came back to the room I asked him, "Where did you go?"

He dipped his head. "I called my parents and to let them know everything that is going on. Mom insisted that we don't have the Sickle Cell trait on our side of the family."

The look on his face told me that they were implying that he may not be my son's father. I didn't know if I should have been angry with him, but that was a very hurtful blow. It had always seemed to me that they thought I was not good enough for their son and that he shouldn't have married me in the first place. I hadn't felt accepted in his family, so this just added insult to injury. Vernal had always tried to assure me that my feelings were wrong. He had said to me once "I think most young ladies think that way about their in-laws." Even though he'd tried to make me not think that way, I still was not able to shake those thoughts and feelings.

But I didn't have the energy to focus on that now. I knew that he was the father of my child. All that mattered to me now was to know what was happening to my baby and how to fix it. I told myself, "Stay focused Narseary, you must stay focused."

I really didn't know what this Sickle Cell business was all about, but from the sound of it, I was sure it wasn't anything good. So I hoped he didn't have the trait and that the doctor's suspicions were wrong.

The doctor finally came back to the room. "Our suspicions were correct. I'm sorry to tell you that your son does have Sickle Cell Anemia."

Oh no! Now, what was going to happen to my baby?

How was I going to deal with this devastating news? I wondered (but for a fleeting moment) what was my husband's family going to think now?

Why did I agree to leave my family and follow my husband to another state? I needed their love and support more than ever.

Lord Jesus, where are you? Can any of this really be happening? Again that overwhelming lonely feeling washed over me. I regretted ever leaving home to come to Connecticut in the first place.

When my husband heard the test results proved positive that he carried the Sickle Cell trait, he had a disappointed and frightened look on his face. I could tell that he felt horrible, scared, and probably a bit guilty. The thought that he may have contributed to his son's illness overwhelmed him, but I felt the same way. His shoulders slumped as tears began to fall from his reddened eyes. He doubled over, wrapping his arms around his stomach.

I was having a hard time trying to wrap my mind around all that was happening.

His parents didn't believe that anyone in their family had the trait. At that time, not many people discussed Sickle Cell, so his family didn't realize they carried it. There were many families who didn't know they had the trait.

I wanted to just get my baby out of there and take us both back home, at least what I considered home-- Rochester. I wanted to get back to my family. I was so scared. How would I ever care for a sick child by myself? I needed my family. I wanted my family.

My head seemed to be spinning around and around. It felt like the floor was about to drop out from under me. *Oh my God, oh God, what are you doing to me? Why God, why? Answer me! Why does my baby have to suffer?*

After Paul had been given some pain medicine, he quieted down enough so that I could phone my parents. My daddy told me that one of his sisters had died from Sickle Cell Disease. I remembered my aunt Bean was very, very, sick when I was a little girl around the age of six or seven. She and her family came to Rochester from Detroit to visit. I remember one day, my uncle and my cousins came to our house and cried. My aunt had died. Until the night that I called to tell my parents about Paul, I hadn't known that she had died from a Sickle Cell Crisis. I also discovered that my father had the Sickle Cell trait. My mother didn't have it though. My mother had four children: three daughters and one son. I, her oldest daughter, and my younger sister have the trait.

The doctor came into the room where we were waiting. They told us that their suspicions were correct and that Paul did, in fact, have Sickle Cell Anemia.

We asked, "What's that?"

He told us, "It's a blood disease that one is born with, and you can only get it if both parents have the trait."

"Oh, God! What in the world do we do now? What does this all mean for my child? Will my baby be all right? Can you fix this? Is there a cure?"

The doctor listened as I fired one question after another before responding. "There is nothing we can do. There isn't any cure. We need to admit your son to the hospital."

Oh God, Lord Jesus, what is going on? I prayed, then cried and prayed some more. My husband just stood there in apparent shock. What in the world were we going to do? *Dear God, What is going to happen to my beautiful child that I had prayed for and waited so long to have?*

Then to make matters worse, I asked the doctor, "What happens to babies who have this disease?"

He looked me in the eye and without blinking, simply said, "They die, and your baby will die too."

No! Not again! Please Jesus, let this not be happening! Please!

Father can you hear me? Where are you Lord? Where are you? I need you! My baby needs you! Help us Lord! Please! Please help us. We need you now!

The next thing we knew, they took my baby to the pediatric unit at the hospital. They needed to insert an IV into his tiny arms, so they kept poking and prodding him, all the while, he screamed, and thrashed trying to reach for me so that I could help him.

Lord, Lord, Lord, what can I do? What can I do? Help my baby, Lord! Tears were streaming down my face merging under my chin forming a river of tears. I was shaking almost uncontrollably with fear. What was going to happen to my baby? He was crying so hard by now. *Oh dear Lord!*

Next, they wrenched him from my arms and put him in a bed with an oxygen tent over him. He kept reaching for me. *Oh Jesus!*

I asked the nurse through my tears, "Why is my baby crying so hard?"

She explained, "He's crying because he's in so much pain. His arms and legs are all swollen because the sickle cells are clogging up his blood vessels."

I asked, "Is there any way you can unclog his veins so that the blood can flow and relieve his pain?"

Shrugging her shoulders, the nurse answered, "No. It takes time. The oxygen tent will help stop the other red cells from sickling too. The sickle cells block the blood flow, and that is what is causing the pain in his little body." That had to have been one of the longest nights of my life.

Since the doctor had told me that there was no cure for Sickle Cell Anemia, the dreaded question kept flying through my thoughts. Finally, I summoned up the courage to voice my biggest concern. "How long will my baby live?"

The doctor answered casually, "Maybe five years, if you're lucky."

What? Lord, Lord, Lord! Please! This could not be happening. I did not just hear what I thought I'd heard the doctor say. No! I must have heard him wrong!

They kept Paul in the hospital for about a week. They stuck my little baby over and over trying to get blood from him and to give him IV fluids. I stayed with him day and night, holding him only when they would allow him to come out from the oxygen tent for short periods of time.

Those were some of the hardest moments of my life because he would not want me to put him back in the bed under the tent. He just wanted me to hold him. I felt so helpless. I could do nothing to take the pain away for my baby.

Lord, I wished that I could take the pain away. Oh Lord, I cried, please help me, and please help my baby.

My husband could not stand to watch them try to get blood from Paul's little arms so he'd leave the room.

I had to hold Paul while they poked and probed to find a vein in his little arms. I tried to fight back tears while listening to his cries, and tried to wipe off both of our tears, all at the same time. What a mess.

Lord, my baby does not deserve this. Why is this happening? I kept asking over and over. I kept telling myself, "This cannot be happening!"

I was really scared when we were finally able to take Paul back home. What was I going to do, when or if, he got sick again?

Before we left, the doctor said, "We'll be seeing you again. This is not the last time your son will need to be hospitalized."

He was right. It was just the beginning of a very long road of hospitalizations and sleepless nights full of horrible pain and suffering. Our lives would never be the same. Not ever again!

Chapter Three

Can I Handle This?

My Paul came home and seemed like his normal fun-loving self. It was so nice to see him playing again. He did not act sick at all. I even dared to think that the doctors must have been mistaken about the diagnosis. I did notice it seemed to hurt him to bend his knees. I think back now, and wonder if he didn't crawl because my little boy's legs and knees were probably hurting and he was not able to tell me then.

Paul began to say words, so I taught him the names of all of his body parts, even ones like elbow, knee, back, and chest. That way he would be able to tell me what was hurting him. I soon found that to be one of the best things that I had done for him.

After God granted my request and gave me my baby, I could see that raising this wonderful and loving being would be harder on me than I ever could have imagined. Sometimes, we should be careful what we ask for; God really does know what is best.

Don't get me wrong. I am so happy that I had my son. I can't even begin to think what life would have been like without him. I was, however, not happy that he would have to suffer the way he did in his short lifetime.

I taught Paul to say the Lord's Prayer when he was twelve months old. He caught on very fast. The world around him excited Paul, and he learned at a rapid pace. He loved going to church. He loved music. He tapped on the table and chairs with pencils. Even at an early age, he tapped with rhythm. It surprised and amazed me to watch him.

For his second Christmas, we bought him a toy Mickey Mouse drum set. He could really pound out a beat. Our friends loved to watch this little kid play the drums with such rhythm.

We bought him a little piano too. His godfather, Chris, used to sit Paul on his knee and played the piano with him and he just loved that.

We would go visit friends and family and Paul would find something to use for drumsticks so he could play anywhere—a coffee table, the chair or even the floor.

Once we were at his godparents' house and his godmother had a plant on top of her coffee table. She had a pencil holding the plant straight in the flower pot. Paul went over and pulled the pencil up and started beating on her table. Needless to say, that didn't go over too well with her.

I learned to carry either two pencils or his little drumsticks in my purse so he'd have something to play with wherever we took him.

Another thing about the pencils was that he'd look closely at them to see if they were both the same size. If they weren't, then he wouldn't want them. He'd cry for different ones. It was amazing to see that even at a young age, he knew the difference.

Once, while we were living in New London, Vernal had taken Paul to the bank with him. The woman standing behind them in line said hello to Paul. When he didn't answer she quipped, "Oh my goodness, it seems as though your little boy is looking right through me." This kind of thing happened a lot.

Once Paul put his hand on someone so I asked him, "Why did you keep touching that lady?"

Paul looked at me and said, "I was praying for her." After that, I noticed he did it quite often.

One day, a little child ran into Paul, causing him to fall down and cut his lip. Since it was a deep cut, I wanted to take him to the emergency room, but my husband just drove us home. I put ice on his lip, and tried to get him to open his mouth so I could check if the bleeding had stopped. He was having no part of it. His little lip was so swollen.

I called the doctor and they told me I was doing the right thing by keeping ice on it, but if he refused to take in liquids, then I should have him checked out. We kept a close watch on him the rest of that day. Later that night, we put Paul in our bed so that I could keep an eye on him, but when I woke up in the middle of the night Paul was gone. My husband went to check to see where he was. He called for me to come to living room, where Paul was standing in front of the picture window staring at the dark starlit sky. We brought him back to bed with us. Later that morning when we all woke up, we checked his mouth. To our amazement, we could not even see where his tooth had cut his lip. The cut was completely closed. He was fine.

When Paul was about three years old, my friend Elisa was having trouble with her boyfriend. She had come over one time after he had beaten her. Paul could see that she was upset and had been crying, and tried to console her.

Still to this day, she tells me that she felt genuine concern from our Paul, and that she will never forget him for that. She was truly touched and amazed that such a young child sensed her pain.

He never stopped having that ability either.

He loved people. It didn't matter who you were or where you came from. It didn't matter the race or position of a person's life. He cared for all people the same. When you were around him, you could feel the love radiating through him. He was so nonjudgmental of others.

Paul was a happy child and really only cried when he was in Sickle Cell Crises. When he was not sick, he was a happy, little boy. It was the hardest thing to see him be so happy and playful one moment, and literally, sick and in pain, the next moment.

My goodness, this was so hard to deal with. How I wished I could stop this horrible cycle of pain. It hurt so much not to be able to do anything. I cannot describe how much it hurt.

My husband had not been able to find a job at first. So I had to get a job shortly after we found out that Paul was sick. We needed to have medical insurance. I was blessed to find a job where my hours were flexible, so if I received a call letting me know that Paul was sick, I could leave to take him to the hospital.

It was hard, so very hard, to leave him with people who did not understand what was going on with him. I remember the sitter really seemed to be good with him, but when he went into crisis while in her care, she thought he was just crying because he wanted me. I came to pick him up one day after work to find dried tears on his face.

I pointed to the tearstains. "What happened to make him cry so much? Look, I can still see the trails of tears on his face."

She waved her hand at me, as if to dismiss my concerns. "Oh, he's fine. He just wanted to be held, and I am not going to hold him all day."

I knew that was not the case with him because he would sit and play with his toys for hours without needing or wanting to be held. I had told her everything before hiring her and clearly instructed her to call me if anything seemed wrong because he may need to be hospitalized. She didn't call because she thought I was just an overprotective first-time mom. Needless to say, I found another babysitter ASAP.

His godmother took care of him for a while since she didn't have any children of her own at that time. Paul's godparents loved him, and they soon were trying to have a child of their own. So she was getting practice, so to speak, by babysitting Paul. She really loved her godson, so that made me more comfortable to leave him with her. She had no problem getting in touch with me if, and when, he seemed sick. Even more importantly, his godmother also believed in the power of prayer.

She did get pregnant and soon was not able to take care of Paul.

By now my husband was working, so I left my job to be able to care for my child. I decided to take classes at Connecticut College. Studying, going to class, and taking care of a sick child kept me busy and was difficult.

There were times when I even took him to class with me. Thank God again, that I had professors who were understanding of my situation and were willing to work with me. Eventually, I had to quit college to stay home to care for my baby, and I never regretted my decision to do so.

Only God knew what was yet to come. That was the best thing that I could have done for both of us. The time between flare-ups lessened as Paul became sicker and required frequent hospitalizations. There were times when the hospital in New London was not able to care for him due to the severity of the crisis he was in, so we'd have to take him to Yale New Haven Hospital in New Haven, Connecticut. I would have to stay over with him in the hospital and not go back to New London until he was discharged. It was difficult for me to work or take classes during that time because my child needed me, and that was all that mattered.

Sometimes we pray for things, not really knowing what we are asking for. I had no idea what was in store for me next.

Chapter Four

Here We Go Again

Since the doctor had told us that Paul would probably not live to be five-years-old, I knew that I did not want to be childless. What the doctor had told us was really beginning to sink in by now. I began to believe that what he said was true and even probable.

I asked the doctor at Yale New Haven what would happen if we had another child. He told me that we could have three more children who would not have Sickle Cell Anemia because only one out of four children would have the disease. Unfortunately, I found out later that that was far from being the truth, and we had not gotten good genetic counseling.

So I started trying to get pregnant, so that when Paul turned two years old, I would be having our second child.

I did get pregnant with son number two. He weighed a whopping nine and a half pounds and we named him King Solomon D. Harris. When I went into labor with Solomon, I told Paul I was going to the hospital for a few days and when I got back home I would be bringing him a baby sister or brother.

When I came home with him, Paul was so excited. All he wanted was "his baby". He hugged and kissed Solomon every chance he got. I really had to keep a close eye on those two.

One time I was in the kitchen and I heard a squeaking sound and shuffling of feet. I turned to look behind me and there they were. Yep both of them! Paul had somehow gotten Solomon up in his arms and was bringing him to me. Oh my goodness, what a scare that was, yet it at the same time so precious. I was breastfeeding and Solomon had started to cry, so Paul brought "his baby" to me so that I could feed him.

Solomon looked like the picture of health—until the unthinkable happened.

At six months, I noticed that Solomon's urine in his diapers was dark yellow, almost brown. He seemed very irritable. He was a chubby baby, but his hands seemed to be swollen. I noticed he was showing similar symptoms to the ones that Paul had when he was at that age.

We took Solomon to the doctor's office that day, only to find out that our Solomon also had Sickle Cell Anemia. Here we go again!

I was sick. No, I was livid!

I could not believe it. Lord! I would not have had another child, if I had I known that he could possibly be sick like Paul. What in the world was I going to do now? What had I done? How could I have been so selfish to get pregnant again? Lord, please forgive me! Lord I'm sorry for getting pregnant again. Please Lord, don't let this happen to this poor, little, innocent baby who had no choice about any of this.

I cannot begin to tell you the guilt that I felt. But one of the doctors had told me that if I had another child the child would not have the disease. What went wrong? I could not believe this was happening to us again.

I was angry at the doctor. I was angry with myself. And yes, I was even angry with God, too. I just could not believe this was happening again.

There were times when both boys were in the hospital at the same time. It was so hard to watch my children suffer such agony. My goodness! How and why did this have to happen? I could not understand this for the life of me. They had to be stuck so many times and because they were so little it was hard to find their veins. There were times I thought I would be physically ill. My stomach started churning. I'd sprint to the bathroom and heave and retch until the bile choked my throat. But I needed to be strong for the boys, so I'd wipe my face, flush the toilet, and plaster a smile on my face and return to their sides.

The years to follow would prove to be some of the most trying times of our lives.

After a while, it got harder and harder to care for my two sick children without the help and support of more family. Don't get me wrong, there were people there in Connecticut that I could call on sometimes, but after a while people start to get tired.

I'm not saying it was a bad thing that some may have felt that way. People have their own lives and their own struggles and tests to deal with. I really did understand that and did not want to be a burden.

So, one of my sisters, Jacquie, moved to New York City to work so she could be close enough to come over on weekends to Connecticut to help me.

She was like a second mom to them. She loved them so much and they loved her. You have to know how much she loved me and her nephews to make such a sacrifice to leave her job in Rochester, New York to relocate where she knew absolutely no one, just to help me. That's love! She had a job transfer, left home, and lived in the YWCA to help me. What a sacrifice. That was just the beginning of many sacrifices she made because of her love for her nephews, for Vernal, and for me.

I was determined not to get pregnant again after Solomon's diagnosis, so I started taking birth control pills. I had negative side effects, however, so the doctor had recommended that I stop them. I had an IUD implanted that got imbedded in the wall of my uterus, so that had to be removed. Then my OB/GYN doctor recommended that I have my tubes tied. While waiting to be scheduled for surgery, we used condoms and vaginal foam to prevent pregnancy. Well needless to say, I discovered that I was one of those women who would get pregnant using condoms and foam. I was so angry, but even more, I was terrified.

I found out that I was pregnant when the boys and I had gone to visit my parents. While we were there, I didn't feel well. I told my mom about my symptoms.

With that special mother voice, she asked, "Hm, do you think you could be pregnant?"

I answered louder than I intended. "No way, we've been so careful!" But when the symptoms didn't subside, my mind flashed back to the other times when I had morning sickness. I decided to go to Planned Parenthood because my doctor was in Connecticut and I needed an answer now. Well, to my surprise and dismay, I found out that I was indeed pregnant. For the first time in my life I thought of having an abortion. All I could think was that I could not take a chance and have another child go through what my two other children were suffering. Lord, what to do? What to do? I was sick with fear of the thought of having another baby. But I could not bring myself to take this unborn child's life. I prayed and asked God if this child was going to be sick, please just let me miscarry as I had done before. Was I being selfish again?

I did not know what to do. I called home to tell my husband that I was pregnant. He sounded happy. What? Was he crazy or something? He said, "Well this could be our baby girl."

I was so angry at him. What in the world was he thinking? Or was he even thinking at all? What was wrong with the man? How could he feel happy about this? Boy, oh boy! Men! I knew he really didn't mean any harm. I think he just really didn't know what else to say.

Even with all that in mind, I could not bring myself to have an abortion. That thought quickly left my mind. Boy, am I ever glad I didn't abort my baby!

I cut our visit short; I drove us back to Connecticut and went to my OB/GYN. He was just as surprised as I was that I'd gotten pregnant again. He was aware of the struggles and changes that we were facing with having the two children with Sickle Cell Disease, and that I was waiting to have my tubes tied.

I was so scared. Unlike the others, this was a very difficult pregnancy. I was sick for most of the time, so I thought this baby might be sick too. Yet I was prayerful, and decided not to worry because I was only making myself more miserable. Besides, there was nothing I could do to change things at this point. I had both Paul and Solomon by natural childbirth. I ended up having to have a C-section with Elijah King James. My husband named all three of our children after kings. I had no idea just how many bumps there would be ahead of us as we embarked on this new phase of life.

Chapter Five

THE BUMPY ROAD

*T*here were times when both Paul and Solomon would have a Sickle Cell Crisis at the same time, so they would be in the hospital together. They both wanted Mommy to hold them, so I'd try. Then there were times when they were not allowed to get out of bed because they needed to be in the oxygen tents, and yet they both wanted me. They would cry until I was able to put one down, and go over to hold the other. Sometimes the pain would be so bad and one would ask, "Mommy, put your hand on my belly." I'd stand for what seemed like hours and if I lifted my hand, I would hear, "No, Mommy, don't move your hand." They would tell me that as long as my hand was on the place where they were hurting; the pain seemed to stop for a while. So no matter how tired I was, I stayed there with my hand on the place of the pain.

While living in New London, we were blessed to have had a very nice doctor for the boys. He was quite attentive to them. He truly cared about their health and well-being.

One day, Solomon felt warm to my touch. I took his temperature and he had a fever. The doctor had told me if the boys' temperature climbed to 100 degrees or higher, then I should bring them right into emergency, but he kept playing, so I thought that he'd be alright. Still though, I phoned the doctor and told him about the fever and Solomon's activities, even though I thought he would be okay, the doctor wanted me to still bring him in.

Solomon was having so much fun outside playing and time got by me. The phone rang and on the other end, the doctor asked, "Why haven't you taken Solomon to the emergency room?"

I said, "Well, he seems to be feeling alright."

"Mrs. Harris, if you don't bring that child in right now, I'll drive over and get him myself!"

You better know, I dropped everything and got him to the hospital ASAP. He did turn out to be okay that time, but Sickle Cell patients can get viruses easily, and something as little as a cold can turn ugly in a hurry. Now that I had another child to care for, it was even more difficult to take care of Paul and Solomon, so we decided to move back home to Rochester, New York, where my parents had found a house for us.

In all the excitement of moving home, I forgot to tell Jacquie, my sister who had moved to New York City to help us. She took the train out to New London like she did every Friday, but we were eight hours away in Rochester.

Boy, was she ever mad at me, and rightfully so. You see, we needed to close immediately on the new house in order to take advantage of my parents' offer. All I thought about was we had to get back Rochester so we wouldn't lose the house. Jacquie didn't want to hear that, because in her eyes it looked like we just up and left without a word to her. Shame on me! After all was said and done, she understood and forgave her big sister. Soon, she moved back home, too. We can laugh about it now, but it wasn't funny when it happened. I really and truly don't know what I'd have done without her.

Oh how I love my sister Jacquie.

After we got back home, we had to find a doctor for the boys. My younger sister recommended her son's pediatrician, so I took the boys there. That turned out to be one of the best decisions I'd make for them.

We found out that the doctor in Rochester, Dr. Webb, had studied at Yale New Haven, and had done an internship with our Connecticut doctor. Dr. Webb was, and still is, one of our dearest and closest friends.

One time, we went to the park for a family cook out. Solomon was about two years old then. We all decided to walk down to the beach area. There were some people listening to music playing from their car radio. He heard the music playing and all of a sudden we heard people laughing. I turned around and he had an audience watching him dance. He was too cute. He was having a ball. We called him the dancing bear because he was so chubby. He grew up to be quite a good dancer too.

Sometimes we really do not know what we are asking for when we ask God for something. He really does know what is best for us, even when we cannot see it. God is a good God.

There were times when Paul and Solomon would seem to be doing well, and then suddenly a crisis would come on. They would look at me and just say, "Mom," with such hurt and pain in their eyes as if to say "No!! Not again. Please help me Mom." Oh, how that would hurt me so because there was nothing I could do to take away the pain. I felt totally helpless. As mothers, we want to keep our children safe from all harm.

Having to trust God during times like that was often difficult. Some people just seem to be able to just take it in stride. I was not able to do that for some reason. I tried hard not to let my children see that it was getting to me though.

As they got older, their cries began to be cries of agony. Sometimes we would wake up to hear them crying out. "Oh God, please make it stop! Mom, come here! Mom!" Vernal and I would jump up out of bed and run down the hall to the room of whoever was in crisis.

Paul was finally ready for pre-school and eager to learn. I still have some of the projects he did there. It helped prepare us for the coming school years. When he turned five, and was ready for kindergarten, we were so excited. He was happy to be going to "real" school. Watching him get on the school bus for the first day was bitter-sweet. Of course I had to go to school that day to make sure everything was going well.

His kindergarten teacher was Mrs. Chris Humphrey, and she was wonderful. She was very mindful of what to look for so as to not let him do things that might make him sick, but yet she let him do the things that would challenge him to learn. She balanced the difficult task of not allowing him to overdo and become sick with challenging him to help him learn.

I remember, one day I waited for him to come home from school, but his bus never showed. The school didn't call to tell me if anything had gone wrong. After about a half of an hour, I called to see if he was still at school and to let them know he had not gotten home yet. The school secretary checked with his teacher and she told her that he was on the bus home. I really got worried then. I jumped in my car and drove over to the school.

 As I drove up to the building, I saw a child sitting and playing in the snow. It looked like Paul so I went over to him. Sure enough, there he was sitting in the snow. I trembled all over when I realized that no one had placed him on the bus. I couldn't fathom the idea that a little boy could slip out and play in the school yard without one person spotting him there. He had been frolicking in the snow, oblivious to the potential danger and to my frazzled nerves. Deciding he would prefer romping in the snow instead of getting on the bus, he scurried around to the side of the school and entertained himself. Because the cold can bring on a crisis, I suspected that he would be ill that night. But thank God, that time he didn't even sniffle.

His teacher apologized and watched him more closely after that. When he would be hospitalized, she would go visit him. That first year of school was trying. One time, Paul went into Sickle Cell Crisis in class. His teacher called me and asked if she should call an ambulance. I told her I would get to the school ASAP to take him to the doctor. He was very sick and had to be hospitalized. Mrs. Humphrey would visit him; tell him about what was happening in class; and read to him. One day she started crying and confessed that she felt she couldn't be strong enough for Paul. As I consoled her, I reassured her how much it meant to us to have a teacher that cared so deeply for our entire family. It meant a great deal to us that she visited him in the hospital.

Later that year, he'd gone into a Sickle Cell Crisis and had been in the hospital for about a week or so.

We thought he was getting better and would be coming home soon. No, not so. Not this time. Things were about to take a drastic turn for the worse. I remember my husband coming home and telling me to call for a sitter for our other two children because we needed to return to the hospital right away. We literally ran from our house to the hospital. Paul was so sick. He had fallen into a coma. The doctors had discovered that at only five years old, some of the blood cells had sickled in a small blood vessel in my little boy's head. He had a stroke at five-years-old.

We stood outside the door to his room. A nurse came from behind the desk and told us we could go in. He was lying there so still. Shortly, one of the doctors came into the room and just stood there. He didn't really say anything that I can remember. He kind of just stood there quietly watching my husband and me sitting by the bedside. He called for the nurse to come back into the room. He told her to remove the oxygen from Paul's nose and to stop the IV. We still sat by his bedside. He was nonresponsive. He didn't seem to even be breathing. I remember asking him, "Where is Dr. Webb?"

He said, "We are waiting for him to come to the floor."

I asked, "What's happening? Why is my baby so still and unresponsive?"

The doctor just stood there looking at us. His face began to turn red and the nurse started to cry. The doctor looked at the clock on the wall and said to the nurse, "We'll wait for Dr. Webb to come and declare him."

All of a sudden, Paul pooped in the bed and tinkled, too. I looked at my baby boy and began to shout his name,

"David? David?" (Until Paul was in high school, we called him by his middle name, David. When he became older, he declared that he should be called by his first name because both he and the Paul in the Bible had suffered a terrible thorn in their sides. He had become involved in the Church Ministry and because of his illness he could relate to the Apostle Paul.)

The nurse put her hand on my shoulder. "Oh Mrs. Harris, please don't do that to yourself."

My husband and I both began to call out his name. He was only five–the same age that the doctors who had diagnosed him had declared he wouldn't live beyond. By this time, my husband and I began to cry, too. The hospital staff, who had grown to care deeply for him, also began to cry with us.

Mom came into the room where we were with Paul. She faced my husband and me, and said, "This is not the time to cry, but to pray! You two stay with David, while the rest of us go into the other room and pray."

My husband and I stayed with our son. We told him how much we loved him. We kissed him. The nurse and the doctor on call told us not to put ourselves through that, but we continued to talk to him. The staff had phoned Dr. Webb to come to his room. They were waiting for him to pronounce our son's time of death. All of a sudden, Paul took a deep breath. Oh my goodness. The staff began running around to get him connected back to the oxygen and took his blood pressure and pulse. When Dr. Webb came to the floor, he made sure that Paul was stable; and then he called one of the larger hospitals where Paul could receive more specialized care. Dr. Webb had thought our Paul had had a stroke and wanted him to get the best care possible. Dr. Webb transferred him to the other hospital by ambulance. After the doctors there checked him over and ran some tests, they did in fact find that Paul had had a stroke at five years old. Yes, our Paul did die at age five. BUT GOD-- gave him back to us. It was a miracle. When Paul was at the other hospital, Dr. Webb went there to be with him until Paul was stable enough to be transferred back to the first hospital.

Paul felt a bit wobbly after the stroke. He couldn't walk straight and felt off-balance but he wanted to go to the play room to play with the other children there. I remember him going to the rooms of the patients who couldn't get out of bed. I asked him, "What are you doing?"

He said, "I'm praying for the kids." He went from room to room praying for the other children on the pediatric floor. Before Paul was discharged, all of those patients that he had prayed for were discharged first. Isn't that something? When it came time for Paul to go home, he was the only patient left on the unit.

He loved the Lord and he would pray and talk to God a lot. Even at a young age. When he was twelve months old, he was saying the Lord's Prayer all by himself. He was a smart little one too. By the time he was in kindergarten, he was reading signs along the road when we would be driving place to place. His teacher told us he was a bright child. As sick as he was, he did not let it stop him. Even at that young age, he had a strong will. No matter how sick he got, he still tried to play.

Both of the boys were like that. They would tell the children that they would be playing with that God was going to heal them so that they could do the things that the other kids could do. They wanted to run, play ball and swim, but when they did they would go into Sickle Crisis.

After the stroke, Dr. Webb did some research and found out that the National Institute of Health in Bethesda, Maryland was hyper-transfusing patients who had thalassemia, which is a hereditary form of anemia, and stroke patients also. He was able to get Paul into one of the trial study program that they were using for some patients. Paul and I would have to make a yearly trip to NIH for years for chelation therapy and to Children's Hospital in Cleveland, Ohio for a liver study which was part of the NIH study. This is a treatment to help remove the excess iron from the blood. It was a painful treatment, but necessary in order for Paul to have the monthly blood transfusions to prevent him from having another stroke. I had to learn how to mix the medicine and then place the needle subcutaneously under the skin in his stomach, thighs, and arms.

Dr. Webb managed to arrange it so Paul could participate in a study at the National Institutes of Health in Bethesda, Maryland. Paul had a stroke at the age of five years old. Oh my poor baby, he suffered so. It amazes me how, even through all the pain, he just kept bouncing back time after time after time. It was simply amazing.

At only age six, Paul joined the School 33 band. His music teacher told us that he had unbelievable rhythm and timing for someone that young. One day I went to the school; she and I were talking about Paul's progress in music class and the band. She said, "Paul's only problem is that he would play all the parts for all of the different instruments on the drums." It amazed me to hear that. He never stopped playing the drums.

We found out just how gifted and talented our Paul really was, both musically and as an artist. We learned that our son had perfect pitch--not relative--but perfect pitch. Paul went from playing rhythms in the air with two pencil sticks to building his own drum set out of a tree branch, tin garbage can lids, and empty paints cans. It reminded me of the old Cosby cartoon, Fat Albert and the Cosby Kids. He went from that to playing a full ten-piece drum set in church.

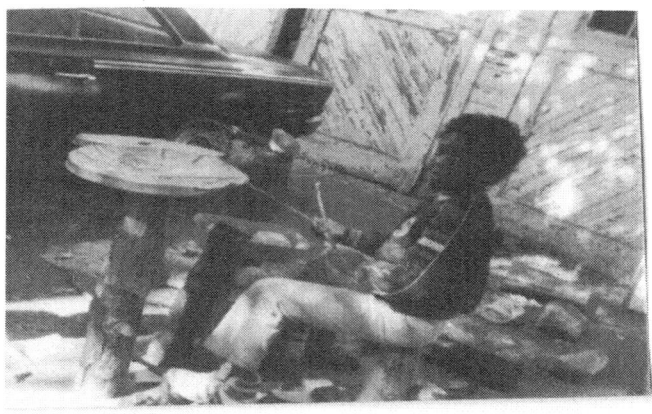

As the boys grew up, they would try to do more and more things on their own. I'd worry about them, but I knew they had to at least try. For a long time they wouldn't even stay overnight with my parents. They wouldn't want to be away from home for long, unless they were sure we would be able to come for them if they changed their minds and wanted to come back home. Solomon especially would not want to be away from home.

They loved to have sleepovers. Our home was the place where their cousins, god brothers, and friends would love to hang out. It seemed I had more children than I gave birth to. After about the second sleepover, I would go to one of my friend's house and sleep there, so the boys could have more fun. I'd leave my husband in charge. Yah right! We know who was really in charge. My husband would go into our bedroom and close the door, and then the boys took over the house.

Their friends had begun to know what to look for in case Paul or Solomon would start to get sick. My nephew, Karl, who was more like my son, would come over most anytime he wanted because my baby sister, Peanut, loved her nephews like her own children as well. They loved her too. She would stick up for them all the time when they got in trouble with me. So, she was one of their favorite aunts. I felt that they were safe with her because she had two younger sons who have Sickle Thalassemia, which is similar to Sickle Cell Anemia.

At about nine-years-old, Paul told me that he didn't want to live anymore. It crushed me to hear him say that. I noticed that he had started giving away his special toys and other things that had special meaning to him.

I was told that that was a sign that a person wanted to die. I tried to give him reasons why he should want to live and not die. The reasons I gave didn't really help him change his mind. I told Dr. Webb what Paul had told me.

He made an appointment for us to talk to a child psychologist. She asked Paul, "Why do you want to die? Don't you know how much it would hurt your mom to see you put into the ground? She would never see you again."

A puzzled look came over his little face. He told the psychologist, "No, that's not what I want to do at all! I don't want to hurt Mommy. If I die, then Mommy won't have to work so hard to take care of me. She wouldn't feel sad anymore or cry when I get sick."

Oh my goodness! All I could see was his love for me. Even though he was so sick, he still was concerned for his mom and the rest of his family. He did not want to be a burden to us. Can you imagine that coming from a little sick child?

I looked him in the eyes. "I'd rather take care of you than to lose you. Everything I do for you is because I love you so much. That's just what moms do. They take care of their babies." I hugged and kissed him and we both felt much better.

We still had hurdles to climb over though. Even today, I cannot imagine the pain and agony that Paul and Solomon were feeling on a daily basis. Yes there were many times that I thought I wanted God to take the pain from them and let me suffer in their place. After all, it was not their fault that they were here. I was the one who kept asking God to let me have children. Surely, I should be the one hurting--not my babies.

Chapter Six

Turning Lemons Into Lemonade

We were told that Paul and Solomon would have a very difficult time in school because they would be sick more often than not. Paul's music teacher recommended him to the World of Inquiry School. That same teacher recommended, and was instrumental in helping, Paul attend the School of the Arts (SOTA). I was so excited and proud of Paul. When we got the appointment for his audition, his proud mother accompanied him. This school was amazing. The students were all so talented and my Paul was going to be one of them. He passed the auditions and was accepted in the School of the Arts for both the music and visual arts programs.

Paul and Solomon had their struggles, but they did not let it keep them from successfully graduating on time. They were in Boy Scouts. Paul played in the school band. They were in school plays. Paul was an Urban League Black Scholar. It was hard to keep up at times, but they were determined to do well in school. I believe they were really bright children, even as sick as they were. When they went to the school of the arts, they each took two majors, Paul: instrumental music and visual arts, and Solomon: drama, and creative writing. They did well. We still have some of their artwork on display in our home now.

Paul and Solomon went camping with their Boy Scout troop, Camp Open Arms, and their youngest brother, Elijah, was able to go along with them. I think that helped Elijah because he was able to see other children who were dealing with sicknesses and see how their siblings coped.

Dr. Webb was going to be attending a camping event with a different troop, and told the boys that he would check on them, which made them feel better about going. Dr. Webb would always check to be sure that the boys were going to have access to the medical treatment availed whenever the boys went on an overnight camping trip. Dr. Webb was amazing. I think it was times like this, when all three of them could do the same things at the same time that helped Elijah to cope with seeing his brothers suffer so much and so often.

I was so afraid to let them go anywhere without me. I really tried not to be overly protective, but it was not easy to do. I knew what to look for in their behavior and mannerism that were signs that they were going to go into sickle crisis. I knew that sometimes they wanted to go somewhere, where the people there may not have been aware of the symptoms and treatment for Sickle Cell Anemia patients. That would give me such a scare. We didn't take many vacations or travel much because I was afraid to be too far away from Dr. Webb.

Once we decided to go south for one of my husband's family reunions. Most of his family had not met our children. I had some reluctance, but agreed to it anyways. I wanted the kids to meet their family and have some family fun. There were already so many other things they could not do. We drove down south and they had a great time. We checked into the hotel. It was so hot outside and Solomon decided he wanted to swim. Oh boy...what was I going to do now? After all, it was so hot out. It couldn't hurt for him to take a quick swim could it? So I consented.

Well, needless to say, that was not the right thing to have done. Solomon got into the pool and began to swim. I noticed that his eyes were beginning to yellow and he had that all too familiar look of pain on his face. Oh boy. I told him to get out of the pool so I could get a better look at him, but he didn't want to get out. The boys always wanted to at least try to do some of the things that other children could do, even if it meant they would end up in the hospital. We were too far from home for either one of them to get sick. We ended up in the emergency room. Of course the hospital staff was not familiar with treating a Sickler. They asked all the normal hospital questions. Meanwhile, Solomon became sicker with each passing moment. I finally asked them to please call our pediatrician back home. Dr. Webb to the rescue! No, he didn't come down south, although I think he would have if he could have. Dr. Webb talked the hospital staff through the best treatment for Solomon and we got on the road, and headed home as soon as Solomon was able to travel.

During Paul's senior year in high school, he was granted a wish through the Starlight Foundation which was to meet Mr. Chuck Morris, who was the drummer for Arsenio Hall's Band, "The Posy." He was a fan of Mr. Chuck Morris, who was, at that time, his favorite drummer. Chuck Morris allowed Paul to sit in and play drums with the band during their rehearsal for the show that day. Mr. Michael Wolff and the other band members were shocked to hear Paul play so well. They were very impressed with his ability to play the drums. They had a real jam session.

Solomon and Elijah were smitten with Starr, who played the keyboard. I don't think she ever knew that though.

We were allowed to take lots of pictures with Mr. Hall and the band members. Mr. Hall took a picture with just him and Paul together. Paul thought that was so cool and he was thankful for that. We were so proud of him. Mr. Hall was nice to Paul. He took us backstage and introduced us to members of his staff, who were all wonderful people. Mr. Hall took time out of his busy schedule for Paul and made us all feel welcomed.

They even taped Paul playing with the band and gave us a copy, which we still have. They gave us special seating for the show and had the camera zoom in on Paul so that all our family and friends back home could see him on TV. That was so cool! They got to meet Teddy Riley who was being interviewed on the show. That was an added unexpected surprise. Denzel Washington was on the show too, but we didn't get to meet him. Paul was hoping to get to meet him after we were told that he was going to be there too. Maybe Elijah, my husband, and I will still have an opportunity to meet him and tell him about our Paul who thought he was an amazing actor. That would be awesome. The Starlight Foundation also gave us tickets to spend a day at Universal Studios during that trip. They had a ball.

Another one of the highlights of the trip was when we checked into the hotel where Paul recognized a TV celebrity who was one the stars from the daytime soap "The Young and the Restless." He played the role of Victor Newman. Paul just went right over to him and asked if he was who he'd thought he was and asked if he would take a picture with him and give him his autograph. Paul was so excited to have met a movie star in the same hotel where we were staying. Paul felt pretty special for sure! Needless to say, the boys had their eyes peeled to see if they would recognize any more celebrities.

The boys had a great time in California. Paul said that it was one of the most unforgettable times of his life. He was so happy and very thankful. And so was I. We had never taken the boys on a real vacation before. I was always too afraid that they would go into a Sickle Cell Crisis and we'd be too far away from their doctor and the hospital staff who knew them so well. Sickle Cell patients can be treated poorly in some hospitals. Sometimes the staff thought the boys were drug addicts, just pretending to be sick to get pain medicine. The thought of the boys going into a Crisis while we were far from home and having to go to an unfamiliar hospital was scary, so the trip to Los Angeles was even more special. Solomon was granted his wish to go on a shopping spree at his favorite shopping mall. He was able to take some of his friends along with him. They were picked up by a limo at his school. Those boys were so funny. Some of the school staff and other students came out to see them off. Solomon thought he was a celebrity that day, and for all practical purposes, in our eyes, he was.

When they pulled up in the mall parking lot, people came up to the limo to see who was going to get out. Someone said, "I think they're Rap Stars." After that, the boys really put on a show for the onlookers.

During Paul's senior studies at SOTA, my husband, Paul's brothers and, I went to a school concert one evening. We were surprised to see that Paul was not playing the drums. After the concert we went up to his music room. I asked, "Hey honey, why didn't you play the drums?"

One of his teachers replied, "We had plenty of percussionists, but we needed someone to play the bass clarinet, so Paul volunteered."

I think my jaw must have hit the floor. "What? Why would he do that? He can't play a horn!"

His teacher chuckled. "Oh yes he can! Paul can play every instrument we have."

I still couldn't believe it. "What? What do you mean?"

His teacher answered, "Whatever instrument we need Paul to play, he just goes over, picks it up, and starts to play it."

On another occasion we went to a visual art display and Paul had some pieces in it. The jazz band was going to play during the event and we were looking forward to hearing Paul play. When we got there and could hear where the sound of music was coming from, I heard the drummer. I told my husband, "Paul must not be feeling well tonight. He is not playing well." I got a bit nervous and wanted to reach him to see if he was in pain. When we got over to the drums, to our surprise, Paul was not playing. We were concerned and found the teacher. "Where's Paul and why isn't he playing the drums?"

He announced, "Paul had decided to play the piano for the jazz band."

Again I asked, "What, the piano?"

He said, "Yes, didn't you know your son could play the piano?"

I shook my head, "Certainly not! Wow! He's awesome!" He never ceased to amaze us. We were so happy and proud of all of Paul's accomplishments in school because this child wasn't even supposed to live past the age of five. Yet at that age, not only did he survive a stroke, but he lived and thrived, scholastically and musically. He had to have his gallbladder removed at 14-years-old due to sickle cell slugging in the blood vessels in his gallbladder. These are just a couple of the challenges he had to endure during his school years, to say the least.

Paul had a hard time during his high school years. His hospitalizations were more frequent. He'd missed a lot of school. People used to pick on him because he stuttered, but he didn't care. His music buddies called him Speech because of it. He took it all in stride.

Chapter Seven

Pain Didn't Stop My Boys!

*A*fter Paul graduated from High School, we had hoped he'd get a music scholarship to college, but he didn't. However, he applied and was accepted at Jonson C. Smith in North Carolina. We were told that there was an excellent Sickle Cell Clinic there; this was why he decided to go there. Of course, Dr. Webb checked things out at the clinic for us. We were all set to take him there, but he got sick. After he was feeling better, he decided he really didn't want to be that far from family.

He then was accepted to and did attend Monroe Community College. This was yet another accomplishment, which Paul had been told would not happen. He majored in music and did quite well. Paul was an awesome artist and musician. We and other family members proudly display his artwork in our homes.

He used to play chess with my dad, who was hard to beat. Paul got good enough to give Daddy a run for his money. He even got good enough to beat my dad occasionally, which made my dad very proud of Paul.

Paul would pray for hours in a day, sometimes all night long. He read his Bible all the way through. I don't know how many times he read it from cover to cover. He had a very personal relationship with God. He wanted everyone he met to know Jesus as their personal Savior. He showed love to everyone he met.

Just before his twenty-first birthday, one of the churches

that Paul played drums with was planning to take a trip. He decided to go. I was kind of surprised that he would go since they were going to Virginia Beach which was a good ten to twelve hour bus ride from Rochester. But he wanted to go and he did. I was so proud of him. He did quite well. By now he would make sure he had all of his meds with him. He knew how to prevent a Sickle Crisis.

Getting cold could also provoke the sickle pain, so when he decided to go on an overnight winter trip with his girlfriend's youth group, I was surprised, but he did quite well that time also. For a short time, both Paul and Solomon worked in the school district. They both substituted as paraprofessionals. Solomon also worked at Burger King. That job was hard for both of them because they had to be on their feet for long periods of time. But no one could ever say that they didn't try; no one could call my boys slackers.

Once, however, when Paul was working at the school, he came to my office. I knew someone had hurt his feelings. He looked healthy on the outside, but often on the inside; he was dealing with excruciating pain. I remember going in to meet with one of the vice principals because of a problem Paul was having at work. I thought because she was a mother she would understand why I wanted her to do something for Paul's working situation. After I shared my concerns with her, she asked, "What good is he to me then?"

I was crushed. I left her office in tears, but I didn't let her see me cry. I went to the principal's office and told him what happened. I don't think he could believe that she would say something that heartless either.

Paul didn't feel well one evening and took himself to the hospital. When he came back home, he had a sad look on his face. I asked, "What's wrong, Paul?"

He said, "Mom, what is going to happen next?" He started to cry.

I put my arms around him and asked again, "What's wrong, Son? What did the doctors say?"

Swallowing back tears, he answered, "I have diabetes."

He felt overwhelmed and devastated. He was planning to get married, and now this. He had a good job with benefits, an opportunity to finish working on his degree in college, which was one of his dreams, and now he had to cope with another serious illness.

Even though he was told he wouldn't live past five, or that he would never finish school, or get married, he refused to give up. So, he kept working, even with this new hurdle called Diabetes. Since his insulin needed to be refrigerated, he would keep his medicine in my office fridge. When he came in to give himself the injections, we'd pray together, asking God to give him the strength to get through the day. He finally became too sick to continue working. He was also married by now, and this was all so hard for him to deal with. He never complained though. He tried to encourage us, even though the illness ravaged his body, and he needed encouragement himself.

Solomon, with the help of one of our church friends, started working at a Rochester museum. He loved that job. He began to have more frequent hospitalizations and was not able to keep up. He went to barber school and earned his Master Barber license. What a great accomplishment that was for him. His friend, who was also an instructor, helped him and stuck by him until he finished the program and graduated. Then, he hired him to work at his shop.

Solomon was still unsure about going too far from home at this point, but some time later, after he married, he moved to Atlanta. He thought being in a warmer climate would help. Things did not go well there and he soon returned to Rochester, New York. He really wanted to move to Los Angeles, but he never made it there to live. The one trip that we took as a family, the one granted by the Starlight Foundation, was the one when the boys did not get sick even one time. Well, if they didn't feel well, they didn't let on. I wish we could have had more family trips together.

Solomon was a writer. He wrote poems about dealing with the pain from Sickle Cell; some of the poems he even wrote music to. He, along with some of his friends and family members, thought he was quite a rapper, which was one of his favorite styles of music. He made a CD with some of his music on it. I asked for a copy, but he said he would have to edit it for my listening because he had some pretty harsh words where it related to his pain and suffering. He never got around to doing it though. He wrote about his love for life and about some of the women in his life that made it a bit more bearable for him during the sickness.

He used to draw picture of characters with big muscles which he wanted to look like when he grew up. He and Paul both used to do that a lot. They, like most little boys, liked and wanted to be "Super Heroes." Even more, I think they wanted to be superheroes because, in their eyes, people like that were healthy and strong, which at that time, they felt anything but big and robust. I tried to encourage them to be all they could and wanted to be. I even encouraged them to be "Super Heroes" because that is who they were to me.

Solomon asked Paul to be Malaya's godfather. Paul loved her so very much. He called her Schoowayly...I have no idea if this is the correct spelling for this name because Paul made it up himself. When Malaya would cry he'd ask her "Schoowayly, why are you schoowayling?" She'd look up at him as he lifted her up in the air and she'd stop crying and give her uncle godfather the biggest smiles. They both enjoyed those times so much.

As the boys grew older they needed a general practitioner, not their pediatrician. We started having a hard time getting the boys to agree to go the hospital. For the first time, we saw firsthand how differently they were being treated after being admitted to the hospital. One time, one of the boys asked the nurse for his pain medication and I overheard her say, "Oh, he can wait; all he wants is pain meds." I felt so angry.

After a while, they would say. "Mom, we may as well stay home and muddle through the crisis rather than to go to the hospital and suffer." This kind of treatment happened most when the staff didn't know the boys personally.

Oh my, the agony on my children's faces, the sounds of their moans and groans was enough to make me want to scream. But I had to hold it together. "Just hold it together Narseary," I would say to myself. "Just hold it together!"

I remember once Paul was in so much pain and he was trying so hard to hold back the tears and not cry out that his eyes became bloodshot. I can't imagine. They told me once that the pain felt like the worst toothache imaginable happening in your legs, knees, and elbows, and sometimes all of those body parts at once. They would be in so much pain, that they would not be able to walk. We would have to pick them up, even as young men, to carry them down the stairs to get them into the car to take them to the hospital. I don't know where the strength to do that came from. Well, yes, I do. I guess I really do know now. It had to be God-given strength.

I'm trying not to feel sad, but I still sometimes get these sick, weak feelings in the pit of my stomach when I think about how they suffered.

In my mind's eye, I can see Solomon sitting on the back porch in freezing cold, winter weather. He would just sit there in the dark for hours.

We would encourage him to come in the house, but he would just nod to acknowledge us and stay out there for a little while longer. I don't know how he was able to stand it. Now, I think maybe his body was beginning to shut down, so he wasn't able to feel just how cold it really was. Normally the extreme cold would send him into a crisis. *Oh Lord...I just don't understand it. I don't. I really, really don't. I don't think I want to try to anymore either.*

I just didn't know how to make the pain go away. Even now, many years later, I still tear up when I think of the suffering my precious babies endured. I just can't help it when I think about them.

I'm trying to think of the good times, and there were some really good times. I just can't seem to stop thinking of the not-so-good times. I want to try to understand all of this. I guess I'm hoping that somehow, some way, sharing my story will help.

We knew some children who had Sickle Cell and were hospitalized a lot during the same times that our children were. One by one they died. At the time that I'm writing this book there is only one young lady that we knew then who is still living. We were told by one of the nurses that she is doing well. Thank God.

Chapter Eight

The Valley Of The Shadow Of Death

I can't think of anything that could have been harder to go through than seeing my son die. It was as though I was walking through a valley of the shadow of death. I felt such a heavy spirit that I couldn't seem to shake. No matter how hard I tried, appearing happy and keeping a smile on my face was excruciatingly difficult. I tried the hardest whenever I was around my sons, during their transitioning period.

I really didn't know that Paul was leaving when he did. He'd been sick, but I thought it was like the other times and that he was going to come home in a few days. About a month before Paul died, he went into the hospital to have an angiogram. I will never forget that day. After the procedure, I walked back to the recovery room to wait with him to be discharged.

When we went in that morning, Paul seemed fine. He walked in on his own and acted like his normal self. What happened after that was the beginning of misery for him.

He was in so much pain. He said, "Mom, it hurts so bad. Please lay your hands on my stomach." He laid there moaning and groaning.

The nurse came in and asked, "How are you doing?"

He told her, "I'm in so much pain."

The nurse shrugged her shoulders. "That's normal after this type of procedure. Let's just give it some more time."

We waited to see if it got better before they sent us home. The pain never got any better, instead it worsened. His abdomen began to swell up. I started to get worried and asked to see the doctor who did the test, but he never came out to see us. One of the attending physicians came out to talk to us. He explained that there may be some bleeding around the area where they tried to access the vessel for the procedure. He left to find a weight to apply pressure to try and stop the bleeding.

After the doctor left, one of the nurses, who had been in the operating room with Paul, entered. She said, "The doctor had trouble threading the scope through Paul's vein in his groin. The local anesthetic didn't numb the area enough. Your poor son almost leapt off the table from the intensity of the pain. I'm so sorry; I'm not quite sure why the doctor didn't give him more medicine."

I felt sick to my stomach when I heard that. "For goodness sake! Why didn't they just stop if they saw it wasn't working?"

She said, "After several tries, they did stop and used the vein in his arm instead."

Oh my goodness, Paul could hardly stand up. I had to help him into a wheelchair to take him to the car. When we got home, it was all I could do to help him climb the stairs to our house, and then more steps to his room.

I walked out of his room to go take my coat off. He called out to me, so I scurried back to his room. He looked at me and I could feel his pain oozing out of every pore.

He asked me, "Mom, what have I not done?"

I grasped his hand. "What do you mean, Son?

His voice wavered. "I fast and pray. I've given my life to the Lord. I have held on to my faith that I would be healed. What have I done wrong? Why won't God heal me?"

I looked at my son and I said to him, "Paul, you have done all that is required of you. Your sickness is not due to anything that you did or did not do. Paul, if you were to die today, your soul would be saved." I leaned in and cupped my hand under his chin. "You need to know that. The devil wants you to doubt God, and to give up your faith. He's trying to sever your relationship with Jesus. Then all your prayers, faith, and pain will be in vain."

He looked me in the eyes. "Okay, Mom."

I wasn't about to give in just yet. "Are you sure you're okay? What made you ask that question right now?"

He attempted to shrug his shoulders and tilted his head. "I'm okay, now. I just needed to know if I am doing something wrong."

I had no idea that my son would die about a month later. He seemed to have a sense of a peace after that, even though his condition worsened each day.

After that procedure, we ended up having to go back to the hospital ER the next day. He tossed and turned all that night. He told his wife that he wished he had not had the angiogram done.

When we came back home from the ER that night, I noticed that Paul did not seem to be himself. A few days later, he went to see his doctor who decided that a nurse should come to our home to check on Paul. He was weakening. Still, I didn't see what was happening-- or maybe I was just refusing to see.

Anyway, the nurse came over one afternoon. After she saw Paul, she asked to talk to me in private. We went out of the room and she said, "Mrs. Harris, I think you should take Paul back to the hospital. I believe a doctor needs to check him immediately."

I told Paul we had to go to the hospital. He agreed without hesitation, which made me think he felt he needed to go too.

The doctor decided to admit him to the Intensive Care Unit to keep a close watch on him. After they got him settled in, his wife and I decided we would stay with him overnight.

Just before everyone else who was still in the room visiting with Paul, he asked me and Shona to come over to sit on his bed. I saw that he was trying to lift his arm, so I helped him put his arm around my shoulder. Then he asked to have help with getting his other arm around his wife's shoulder. He looked from side to side at the two of us and said, "Now we are all together."

I said, "Yes, we are." Knowing that the two of us were there with him seemed to comfort Paul. The boys always wanted me to stay with them when they were in the hospital because they knew I would ask all kinds of question when the doctors came in to see them. If they were in pain, they knew I wouldn't hesitate to call for their pain meds. And if I thought for any reason that they were not being treated right, I had no problem speaking up. That knowledge gave them a sense of peace and helped them rest as much as was possible under those circumstances.

Dr. Harris (no relation) came in to see him. She checked him over and said. "I'll see you all in the morning."

Just as his wife and I got comfortable in our chairs, one of the nurses came in to give Paul some medications. His breathing sounded funny. He would inhale deeply, and then breathe faster, followed by a gradual decrease of breaths. I pointed this out to the nurse. "Why is he breathing like that?"

She tossed her hands in the air. "Well, what do you want me to do?"

Blinking back surprise, I answered, "What do you mean?"

She said, "You need to let me know if you want me to crack his chest."

I asked her, "Why would I want you to do that?"

Red patches covered her cheeks. "You don't know do you?"

I could feel my heart beating faster. "Know what?" All of a sudden, reality smacked me in the face and I shouted, "Go get my husband!"

"Where is he?"

I pointed to the door. "He's in the waiting room."

She ran out, but by the time they got back it was too late. They found me holding my Paul's hand. I had watched him take his last breath.

His wife looked at me and said, "What just happened?"

She sat there with this bewildered look on her face. Neither of us could believe what had just taken place right before our eyes.

Before I knew it, the room was filled with family and friends. I, still to this day, don't know how everyone entered his room so fast. The days after that were such a blur.

It has been twelve years now and I still can hardly believe it. I don't know if I will ever forget that moment. This child that I'd prayed for, after only 26 years, had died right before my eyes. *Oh my Lord why, why, why? I don't understand! Why?* I cannot describe the feeling I felt at that moment. My mother came over and sat near me. "Mommy, pray and ask God to give him back to me." I begged, "You did it before when he had the stroke and died. God put life back into his five-year-old body, so He can do it now too! Pray!"

She looked at me and said, "Not this time, Seary, not this time. He's gone Narseary. Our Paul is gone."

The hospital staff called for Dr. Harris to come back up. She just stood there for a moment. Then she looked at me and said, "I was looking forward to see him eat his breakfast in the morning."

I really and truly did not expect my child to die that night. I just was not at all ready for that. I couldn't understand why God didn't let me know that was going to happen. Why didn't He tell me that He was going to take my son to Glory that night?

You see Paul and Solomon had been in the ICU before so the staff could carefully monitor them. I didn't think this time would be any different. Lord, I was just not ready for that! I have to say though, that it was very strange that night. So many people came to visit him. Some who I didn't even tell he was in the hospital rushed over. One in particular was one of my friends whose daughter had passed just a few years prior. Her daughter also had Sickle Cell Anemia. I don't know why she was there. The waiting area was filled with our family and friends, who for some reason had not left the hospital.

I wish I had been able to tell Paul that it was alright to leave. I wish I had sung a song or prayed a prayer with him. I was just not ready to say goodbye to my Paul. He just slipped away. He used to suck his tongue and that's what he was doing. He just lay there, quietly, restfully, and peacefully, with me and Shona on either side of him. As I held his hand, I watched my son take his last breathe. I could not believe it. My wonderful son was gone. He had so much left that he wanted to do. His songs were waiting for him to produce them. He had sermons he wanted to preach. He wanted to have babies. *Lord, why couldn't he have gotten to do all those things?*

What had made me so angry was that it wasn't the Sickle Cell Disease that took his life. After all the suffering he went through with that disease, and it ended up not being the cause of his death. The side-effects of the angiogram, that he really didn't even need, claimed his life.

It angered Vernal to know that a mistake had been made, so he went to see an attorney to see if we could do something about it. We signed papers to have Paul's records released to the lawyer and after reviewing them, they called us in to tell us they had discovered some negligence during the procedure.

They also told us that it would be very costly to go to court with it. The lawyer said there was documentation showing that Paul was going into renal failure as well. He told us because of that, a jury could decide that my Paul was going to die anyway and rule in favor of the doctor and the hospital. I told my husband that I didn't know if I could handle someone telling me that they would rule in the favor of the doctor who did something that caused my child's death. I didn't care if he would have lived for only one more month. That would have been a month longer that we would have had with him that was taken away from us. Only God can grant peace through a test of faith like this one.

There were over a thousand people in attendance for the memorial and home-going services held for our Paul. The then mayor, Bill Johnson, and other prominent people were there and had words in memory and honor of our Paul. People, to this day, still tell us that they had never witnessed such a powerful memorial and home-going service.

Many people still tell us how Paul did a kind deed or how he had prayed for them.

I have never met anyone quite like him, and not just because he was my son, but because he was someone special.

At the memorial service, the spirit was so high and the choir sang with such joyous praise. Paul loved praise and worship. I was looking at him in the casket and I saw his body moving. At first I thought, "Oh My God. You are going to raise Paul from the dead right before all these people and they will see your mighty power and believe on you and Paul will be healed." That is what I was truly thinking. I didn't say anything to my husband because I didn't think he saw what I saw and I didn't want him to think I was so stressed that I was imagining it.

Well, at the home-going service the next day, that mayor was reading his proclamation. He stopped in the middle of it and said, "I was at that service last night and I don't know if anyone here saw what I saw. My father was a mortician and I was raised watching my father in his business. I know that when a body is dead and lifeless it does not move, but last night, I saw this young man's body moving and lifted out of the casket. It seemed like he was letting the choir know that one last time, he was there singing with them!"

We found out that others also saw that too. It was truly amazing!

I felt that we were walking through the valley of the shadow of death; and we were, but discovered that God walked every step right next to us. He brought me and my family through those hard and difficult times.

Chapter Nine

What a Trooper

We had two sons who had Sickle Cell Disease. I gave birth to both of them, and yet they had two very distinct personalities. The effect that the illness had on them was very different in terms of their responses to it.

My Solomon's passing was as unique as my Solomon's life had been. He tried hard to hold on to life. He didn't want to leave his children. He wanted more time with them. It was nearing the time when Solomon was passing. He was still home with us. It was just days before he would have to be taken to hospice. The doctor had come over to check on him. She could see that he was leaving us soon.

Solomon had asked me to run to the store to get him some more body powder. He was quite specific about the brand he wanted. I thought it was because he liked that fragrance the best. I also thought he was going through quite a bit of powder too. When I found out he was eating it, I was very concerned for him. I told his doctor that he was eating the powder and she told me it wouldn't hurt him because his body likely lacked some minerals, so he would crave the powder to provide what his body needed. Isn't that funny how that works? So from then on, I stopped bugging him about eating it.

One afternoon I helped him get to the bathroom. When he was done he called out for me to come in to help him back to bed. When I opened the door, he was sitting on the toilet and leaning forward. At first I thought he was falling over. I hurried over to help him up, but he stopped me and said, "Here, read what I wrote."

I saw a big mess of body powder on the floor in front of him. It read "I didn't eat the powder." All I could do was laugh. Clearly he'd been eating it. I think he must have been eating it when he dropped the container and decided to write me a note in the spilled powder. He knew he would not have had the energy to clean it up himself, and I guess he figured that would be a better way for me to find the mess he'd made. That was one of the funniest things I'd seen him do in a very long time. But I still knew it wasn't a normal thing for him to have done. He was very fussy about things being neat around him. Oh my! I miss him so much right now!

He had a strong, loud voice which got down to a mere whisper. He was so thin.

One night, Elijah and I were in the bedroom with him. We had just gotten him changed and repositioned to be more comfortable. He started to stare at the doorway. He was laughing. Elijah asked, "What's so funny?"

He said, "I'm laughing at Paul." Well, Paul had been gone to Glory for ten years at the time. Elijah and I looked at each other.

Elijah asked Solomon, "What's he doing?"

He said, "He's just standing there looking at me. He wants me to come and go with him, but I'm not going with him. He'd better come over here and eat with me."

Solomon wasn't eating. Elijah and I stood there looking at each other. Elijah asked, "What is Paul wearing?"

He answered, "He's wearing his black suit, like he's

getting ready to preach or something." Solomon smiled. "I'm not going with Paul. I'm going to wait for God, and when he comes I'm going with him."

He stopped smiling so I asked, "What's Paul doing now?"

He said, "He's gone now. You just missed him."

A few days later, the hospice doctor came to the house to check on Solomon and told us she thought we should let her call for an ambulance to bring him to the hospice facility. At first, I didn't want to because I knew Solomon didn't want to go there. He had rejected hospice for a long time because he'd thought going there would mean he was going to die and he was not ready for that.

But Elijah said, "Mom, I think we should let them take him."

I nodded. "Okay, maybe they can make him more comfortable and it is getting harder for us to move him."

I am so grateful and thankful for Hospice Buffalo. I really don't know how we would have gotten through those last few days with our Solomon without their help and support. Hospice care was nothing at all like we had thought it would be. They were wonderful.

His father preached Solomon's home-going service. During the service, Vernal had asked someone to place two chairs up front facing him. He asked Elijah and me to come up to sit in them. He said, "It's just the three of us now. We were there for Paul and Solomon, and now we have done all we could for them. We have done our best. I know that the boys believed that we did everything we could as their mother, father, and brother.

Now, they would want us to move forward with the knowledge that they appreciated us and that they loved us deeply."

It has been a long and hard twelve years trying to go on without Paul and three without Solomon. It still feels like just yesterday that they left. Yet, I have come to know they will never really leave me; they will forever live on in their mommy's heart. I still see your smiles. I still feel your hugs. I still see you in my dreams. You will always be a part of me.

"After Life"
An Original Writing by: King Solomon D. Harris

I do not fear death.

Why should I fear that which would allow me to once
again see a lost brother who I miss and loved so dearly, a
sister I never had a chance to meet, and my Savior and
Maker for whom I have an infinite amount of unanswered
questions, and escape from a life of pain!

Fear death? No, I await death.

Don't feel sorry for me...envy me. You see death as
something bad and evil. You run and hide from it as if
you could escape if it were to come for you anyway.
Cowards! You find something in your life to complain
about every day, and then see death, the only escape from
all of life's tribulations, as something horrific.

Not I, especially when me and pain are of the same breed.
Me and pain are one. No, I take great comfort in knowing
that eventually me and death will finally meet. And so
should you. So no, don't pity me, just pray for me!

Chapter Ten

After the Dust Settles

*S*o, I ask, how do I go on from here? I really don't know sometimes, how I can. I know I must, but how is my question. I think I'm making progress at times. I still have moments when it feels like I'm stuck in time. I feel so lost. I try to see the light at the end of the tunnel. Sometimes it seems clear and close. Other times it seems very far away. There are days when my thoughts are clear and the details are flowing through my thoughts. I come over to my computer and begin to write and I think I'm doing okay, only to discover that the thoughts have trickled away, much like sand through my fingers. There is so much I want to share. So many memories that I know many of you can identify with. I want to give you hope, to encourage you and to reassure you that you will be alright. I know there are moms reading this book and tears are flowing down their faces. Your heart is hurting and you are asking God why. I just want you to know that you are not alone in your struggle with these feelings. There are so many of us who feel your pain. We all deal with them in our own way, but the pain is real and we must find peace, the kind of peace that only God can give. Oh, and I know that there are times when you don't think that God will give you that peace. I know because I have been in that dark place many times myself. I'm holding on with a tight grip, even now. The memories of our children will be with us forever. Don't think that you will ever forget your child. You never will forget. I try to think about fun times. Even thoughts of the fun times can sometimes hurt. Isn't that funny how that happens? But it's true.

Words cannot express the hurt and loss I feel knowing they have passed on. Yes, I know they are in a better place. I'm sure of that...I just miss them being here with me right now. Paul and Solomon were both almost six feet tall and I'd tell them at times when they would be at home to come over here and sit on your mommy's lap. They'd shake their heads and smile as if saying "Mom you are so silly;" then would come and gently sit on my lap in my rocking chair.

The passing of his brothers has impacted Elijah's life and influenced a lot of the decisions he's made; some for the best and some not quite so good. He is now trying to turn some things around in his life, so that he produces good music. His brothers were so proud of his music. They both want him to be a successful music producer and he is doing that.

My youngest son (Elijah) went to his doctor for an annual physical and she told him that he was suffering from "Survivor's Guilt Syndrome." She advised him to talk with a counselor about it. It has been very difficult for him. He was just a little boy, when his brothers went into crisis and had to be hospitalized. Elijah would take his pillow and blanket to the bedroom of the brother who was in the hospital and sleep on the floor next to their bed. There were times he'd seem to feel even sadder than others and I wondered what the difference was in one hospitalization versus the others. Later, I discovered that Elijah was feeling guilty for not being sick too. He felt bad that he was able to do things that his brothers couldn't do like go swimming, play basketball, football, and even run for long distances. I don't think he really understood that they wanted him to do all the things that they could not. They enjoyed watching him play sports.

Elijah immersed himself in music. Carl Thomas helped Elijah by allowing him to escape into his music, which allowed Elijah time to grieve in his own way and at his own pace. God really has a way of ordering our steps even when the way is dark and dreary. Carl was there for Elijah, and then later, when Carl found himself in the midst of a tragedy, Elijah consoled him too. Carl's oldest brother tragically died in a drive-by shooting. Carl told me, "Mom, I am glad Elijah was here when this happened. I was able to talk to him and knew he really understood my pain because he lost Paul. "They both knew how to comfort the other, either through words, prayer, or just being there to listen. They understood that grief is not a sign of weakness, but a way to heal and move forward. At the time that Carl brother past

Solomon was still alive.

At times along this journey, I found that I felt bitter and angry. Still, I have moments of sadness, but I know that if God brought us through that, He will be here to get us through on the next phase of our journey.

I still don't want to go to the cemetery where Paul is buried, but it seems to help my husband and Elijah to go there, so I go with them sometimes. It still makes me sad. Solomon didn't want to be buried because he didn't want his dad to go to the cemetery and cry over him the way he did for Paul. He asked to be cremated. It still hurts the same though.

I have truly found out that God is able to see me through. He promised never to leave. He promised that in every trail He would make a way of escape for me so that I would not yield to the temptations that come through by way of the test.

(I Corinthians 10:13 KJV) *"There hath no temptation taken you but such as is common to man: but God is faithful, who will not suffer you to be tempted above that ye are able; but will with the temptation also make a way to escape, that ye may be able to bear it."*

Through every test that my sons went through, they both, like Job, refused to curse God and die. They chose to trust Him even in death. They waited for their change to come. Now they are in glory.

KING

SOLOMON D.

HARRIS

Accomplishments of
Min. Paul King David Harris

1986 – 1992

Attended School of the Arts and graduated majoring in Visual Arts, Drama, Instrumentation, Music Major

1988 – 1989

All City Jazz Band, All City Concert Band

1989

Drums & Percussion for Musical, Gospel and West Side Story

1989 – 1990

Hochstein School of Music (Drums, Steve Curry, Instructor)

1992

Rochester Urban League Act-So Bronze Medalist

Appeared on Arsenio Hall Show through the Starlight Foundation and played drums.

1994

Black Gospel Instrumentalist of the Year

1994 – 1997

Musician for Monroe Community Choir Gospel Choir

1995

Organist-Keyboardist for Spirit Inc. Choir (1996 Black Gospel Music Awards Choir of the Year)

Accompanied Edwin Hawkins on Keyboard

1995 – 1996

Minister of Music at Power House COGIC

1996

Provided Music on Divine Nature Demo CD Song: "You are a part of me" presently playing on radio

Produced music for "The Profitz" Demo

Accompanied "Uneek" on keyboards at Tina Watson of the Grammy Award winning Thompson Community Singers

1997

One of Four Choir instructors for Annual Martin Luther King Concert

Minister of Music at Triiinity Temple Church of God in Christ

Produced and Programming music for "Dr. Rock"

Accompanied Dorinda Clark-Cole on piano at Holy Convocation

1997 – 1999

Producer for Dajhelon Entertainment Group

1999

Founded Holy Ground Music studios and performed during the summers of 1999 and 2000 at the Kingdom Bound Festival. He also was employed with the Rochester City School District. In 2000 he was licensed as a minister in the Church of God in Christ, Western New York Jurisdictional #1

Don't stop believing. Don't give up. Stay focused. Don't allow the test to distract you from your purpose. God knows just how much you can bear. In Philippians 4:13, it states, *"I can do all things through Christ which strengtheneth me."*

I know you feel like throwing in the towel. I felt that many times. I thought I would not make it through to the next day. But God brought me through. I give Him all the glory. *All the glory belongs to you, O God.*

So how do I go forward without my two sons? I don't, because they are forever with me in my memories. They will always be a part of me. I still dream of them. I have my husband and my youngest son Elijah; and the three of us have a part of Paul and Solomon that they left with us. I have two beautiful grandchildren that Solomon gave me. I have family and friends who still remind me of times that Paul and Solomon made them laugh or did something that impacted their lives. The love they gave to me, as their mom, gives me the strength to share their story so that someone else will know that they, too, can move forward. I still think, "Did I really have them?" I know I did, but it sometimes feels like a dream. They were such strong young men. With all the horrible suffering, they still found a way to laugh, sing, and love. They weren't angry and bitter people, but loving and kind. How did they manage to give so much strength to others through all that pain? They gave me so much, and I sometimes feel that I didn't give them enough.

My boys had such strong will and determination. They were determined to beat the odds. Paul became the musician, song writer, and music producer that he had dreamed of being. He went to college, which was another thing he was determined to accomplish. He resolved to stay in the will of God, preaching and teaching His word, no matter what, even when it meant doing it from his hospital bed. That is determination.

In Solomon's senior year in high school, they had met with a recruiter from the military. Solomon had admired two of his cousins (Ken and Randy Jr.) who had joined the Marine Corps. He thought they were real tough. He had wanted to join the United States Marines like they had. I told Solly that I didn't think he would be able to do that.

He came home from school one day and announced, "The recruiter is coming over to our house this afternoon."

I asked Solomon, "Why is he coming here?"

He said, "I think he wants to talk to you about me going into the Marines."

I tossed my hands up in the air. "I don't think they will allow you to go into the Marines because you have Sickle Cell Disease."

He shook his head. "I can do it Mom!"

When the recruiter met with us, I found out the gentleman was not just there to talk. It turned out that my Mr. Solomon had enlisted himself in the Marines. Yep! That Solomon was determined to become a Marine. I just sat there listening to what they had to say.

Finally the recruiter said, "Okay, Solomon, now all we need to do is get your physical done and we will be on

I looked at the gentleman. "Has Solomon told you about his health problems? He has Sickle Cell Anemia."

He looked at Solomon and shook his head. "Why did you leave out such an important piece of information?"

Solomon just looked at him with a big smile on his face. "Because I know I can do it."

No, Solly wasn't able to enlist, but he sure tried. He was determined to do whatever he set his mind to do. He was not going to let that illness stop him if he had anything to do with it. Those boys never gave up on their dreams; so they wanted Elijah to pursue his dreams too. They wanted to play sports in school, but couldn't. Well, once again, my Solly had one of those "I'm going to do it anyway and Sickle Cell is not going to stop me" moments. He joined one of the neighborhood community center's football teams in Rochester. I will never forget one day when we all went to watch Solly practice for a game. One of the things the team had to do was run around the whole field. We knew that was going to be very difficult, if not impossible, for Solly to do. We had already told the coach about Solomon's limitation due to his illness, but Solomon had asked me and his dad to please let him try.

We had to say no to so many things the boys wanted to do, so this time we agreed. We told him he had to promise to let us know when he was not feeling well right away. He promised to do that. Both boys would try to hide their pain if it meant they would have to stop doing something that they really wanted to do. That was not a good thing though. But they just wanted so much to be able to do the normal kinds of things that their family and friends did. Well, all the boys on the team started to run around the field. There was a tall hill on the far side of the field and we weren't able to see the kids at that point. One by one, the boys would come around the hill. We waited and waited to see Solomon come around. A few minutes went by, but no Solly. We began to get worried, and just then, we saw Solly slowly jogging in. I could tell he was sick. His dad tried to jump the fence to run out on the field to get him, but the coach stopped him. They had an ambulance on site, just in case they were any problem with any of the boys. Thank God. Next, he had to go to the emergency room at the hospital. Solly had gone into a Sickle Cell Crisis and needed to be admitted.

The coach felt bad, but we assured him that all was well and thanked him for giving our Solomon a chance to try. After the football game, the coach and the entire team came up to the hospital to visit Solomon. They won that game and they brought the football up with them and told Solomon that they won the game for him. How cool was that? Solomon gave them his big Solomon smile.

Solomon was very political too. He ran for political office and won twice. It was amazing to sit and watch the polls come in. When he was around six years old, he was the Sickle Cell poster child in Rochester.

Solomon was in the hospital the day his son was born. When he found out that his wife had come to the hospital in labor, Solomon told his doctor that he had to go over to the labor room to be there when his son was born. He was determined to be there for his birth. It didn't matter how much pain he was in; he was going to be there.

So Paul and Solomon were so happy when Elijah decided played football his senior year in school. They told him, "Do it for us Elijah." They were so proud of him.

They wanted him to become the successful music producer that he wanted to be. Elijah immersed himself in music. No matter how we lose a child, it hurts. The pain of your child being taken from you way before they reach adulthood is devastating. We just never are prepared for it. I don't know if anyone who has not lost a child can truly understand the pain.

I lost my dad, but that was a different pain all together. I miss him dearly. When problems come in my life that I have a hard time dealing with, the little girl in me wants to reach out for my dad. The thought of him not being there is sometimes overwhelming. Still, it is a different pain from the pain of losing my children. However, wherever and through whomever the pain comes, when losing a loved one, the pain and sadness is there and it is real. The thought of never seeing them again can cause agony and hopelessness in one's life. But please don't give in to those thoughts and feeling. I know it may be easier said than done, but I am here to tell you that you can make it.

How do I go forward without them? I don't. They are right here and always will be with me! And so will your loved ones be with you.

Chapter Eleven

There is Hope

*T*here was a profound peace that came over me during a home-going service that I'd attended some years ago. It was for a young girl who had also died from Sickle Cell complications. Someone shared with the bereaved family that God was in control. They said that whenever you plant a seed in the earth that it must grow. They assured the family that it was genuinely hard to say goodbye to their daughter, but just as sure as the seed was planted, (their child as a result of burial) that seed would grow. I pondered those words for a long time. Now, I know what was meant by them. I now know that as a result of my boys passing, the seeds of their lives are now planted in the grounds of time; they too will produce a harvest.

I know that because there are still people being blessed by their memories of my sons. I pray that everyone reading this book will be blessed and that in whatever sorrow or testing of your faith, you will gain strength and courage to move forward. We cannot let our past dictate (in a negative way) our future.

The cover of my book was inspired by a canvas painted about three years before I began writing our story.

During my Annual Women's Conference I brought in an Elder of the Gospel by the name of Richmond Futch. He is an awesome artist. He would paint under the anointing of the Holy Spirit during the praise and worship service on the Sunday closing of the conference. During the service, there would be a silent auction and the highest bidder would get the painting that afternoon. For years I'd wanted to get one of the canvases, but someone would always outbid me.

Well, the year that Solomon passed, no one outbid me. I was so excited that I was finally going to have the original canvas that year. I left it in my office at the church for months. On one particular occasion, while sharing with someone who had come to my office about my conferences and the gift of ministry that Elder Futch brought to the conference, I remembered that I had the canvas in my office. I pulled it out to show the individual. As I was looking at the canvas, I realized that the painting seemed to look like it was representative of my three sons standing in the middle of a broken heart. The theme for that year's conference was "Search Your Heart." Then I took a second look and thought, "No that is me, my husband, and my son Elijah standing in the mist of the broken heart." The drops of blood from the broken heart seemed to be sickle cells which were falling to the ground, and as a result they caused grapes on a vine to grow. I began to cry because I knew that God was letting me know that the words that I had heard the year before were coming to pass for me; and truly, the seeds of my sons' lives were going to produce a harvest. Oh bless the name of the Lord. God is so faithful. Don't give up! Don't give in. The best is yet to come. Through your test come testimonies of the greatness of our God.

There is hope for us as we try to move forward. There is hope because we serve a Savior who is now sitting on the right hand of His Father, interceding to Him on our behalf. He knows what we are going through and He knows how difficult it is. Jesus and His disciples went to be with Mary and Martha, whose brother Lazarus had passed. John 11:35 says, *"Jesus wept."*

You have to know that it really is alright to cry. I know we feel that we have to be strong for others, and in some cases we do. You still have to know that you too have to go through the grieving process. We do not all react to death the same way and that is okay too. If people don't feel comfortable around you during a difficult time, you should not try to hold your feelings in. It is okay to leave the environment until you are feeling better. God will give you a shoulder to lean on. I know His shoulders are broad and wide. Yet, and still, He will give a human shoulder also because we gain strength from one another. Isn't God good? Yes He is!

It's okay if you don't always feel like putting on that happy face for other people. God will bring people into your life that will mourn with you. During the Sermon on the Mount, Jesus told His disciples, *"Blessed are they that mourn: for they shall be comforted."* (Matthew 5:4 KJV) It was not an easy task for Him to be beaten and scorned. He endured the lies, the torture, and the open shame and humility just for us, and as a testimony to us that, with Him, we can and will make it.

My sons made it. They stayed the course. They didn't let anything come between them and their relationship with God. They taught me a life lesson that I can make it. No matter how hard and challenging life may be, I can make it. I know that no matter what I'm going through, it is only a test.

The boys had a dream that they would be instrumental in finding the cure for Sickle Cell Anemia. They wanted to meet Oprah Winfrey and Tboz, one of the singers in the group TLC, who also has Sickle Cell Anemia. They'd hoped that these two awesome women would champion their cause for the cure. Perhaps I'll get to meet these inspiring women to share more of my sons' stories with them. Who knows? All things are possible to them who believe.

I will always miss my Paul and Solomon. I'm thankful for the beautiful granddaughter and the handsome grandson that Solomon gave us. They look like their dad and they miss him. I know there'll be moments in their lives when they will hurt and wish he could be here with them. I try to be there for them, but I know I'll never be able to fill that void. When they talk about their dad now, they remember the fun times. It's healing for me to hear them laugh about something he did or said. Solomon wrote Malaya (his daughter) a letter telling her how much he loves her. She put it over her bed. In a way, I thinks she feels that he is there watching over her. Solomon Jr. loves to hear that he is like his dad. He gets the biggest grin on his face. Solomon really loved Malaya and Solomon Jr. He would hug and kiss them or sometimes he would just sit quietly with them as if he were taking in his last glimpse of them. Then he'd ask them to come closer so he could hug and kiss them some more.

How do I move forward without them? I know now that I don't. They will always be a part of me and what I do for kingdom building.

Chapter Twelve

Thank you to Family and Friends

*T*here are some very special people who we were blessed to have been a part of our journey. I really don't know what we would have done if they had not been there for our immediate and extended family. They loved and cared for my boys in a way that words can't describe. They brought joy and faith into our lives and they meant so much to my boys. I know this because Paul and Solomon told me so. I loved to hear them reminisce about the fun times they had with some of these wonderful people. They were, and still are, a blessing to me as well.

Shawn's children call me Aunt Seary and my sons called her Aunt Shawn. She is a very dear friend to me and my family. Her first grandchild passed at a very young age. She knows the devastation and pain of having a child pass. I was with her and her daughter when her granddaughter took her last breath. As I remember, Paul was there too. Shawn traveled to Bethesda Maryland with Paul and me for several years. She spent countless hours sitting with the boys and me during their many hospitalizations. I truly thank her for her consistent love and support. Shawn is a cancer survivor, yet she gives so much of herself to help others.

Aunt Dee is a very dear friend, who is more like a sister to me. The Lord brought her into our lives and I am so glad that He did. She used to get so upset when the boys would get sick and she didn't understand why I still gave God glory in spite of it.

She would ask me, "How can you trust in God when he allowed your children to suffer?"

With a slight smile, creeping across my face, I answered, "I know that God is fully capable of healing them. For that reason alone I trust him. Even if His will is to not heal them, I still believe he has a plan in all of this that is far greater than we, as humans, can even begin to comprehend. Somehow, some way, I know God will use my boys to bring Glory to His name. What a blessing that He has chosen our family to experience this, so that someday our pain will not only glorify Jesus, but also may lead a lost lamb back into the Shepherd's care!"

She grew to really love them. One hot summer day, she came over to visit. "Boys, how about coming with me to the community pool for a quick swim?" The problem was the boys would need to jump over the locked fence at the community pool.

I raised my eyebrows. "Dee, no they can't do that!" She was so silly. She would come up with the most spontaneous, fun things for them to do. Well, since I wasn't going for that she decided that they should spray each other with the water hose. Then I guess she thought they weren't getting wet enough, so she went and bought balloons and filled them with water and they had a balloon fight. Well that wasn't good enough either, so they came inside the house and they all started throwing pots filled with water at each other. I thought, "Oh my goodness, what in the world is she doing?"

She looked at me and said, "Well, now you have a clean floor." She started laughing so hard and so did the boys.

I am so grateful that Dee came into our lives. She loved

the boys, and always made them laugh. With her, they had some of the best times of their lives. They never forgot it. She would go to the hospital, sit with us, and hold our hands during the difficult days. Even now, she is still here for Vernal, Elijah, and me. Thank you, Dee, for being a friend, who is like a sister, to me.

All in all, we were truly blessed to have doctors and nurses who cared for our children, not just as patients, but as family. They took time to listen to them and tried to understand their pain. When they were pediatric patients, the staff would really look after them when I was not able to be there or until I got back to the floor if I had to leave for some reason or another. They really and truly cared about them. It would be nothing for Dr. Webb to come by our home to check on the boys on his way home from working at the hospital. He even came to Paul's high school graduation and sat with our family. He would also later attend Paul's funeral. We love you and thank you, Dr. Webb.

Deidre, my childhood friend, was a loving godmother to Paul and a great support system for me and Vernal. Her timely phones calls and words of encouragement have been a true Godsend. Thanks for sharing your daughter and my beautiful goddaughter, Kyndra, with me. Even when I was pregnant with Paul, you'd bring her over for me to babysit her. I still feel that she is my baby girl (young lady) too. Thanks Kyndra for being there for your god brother Elijah.

Karen is one of my closet friends as well. She and her family are like family to my family. When Paul passed, she left work to come over to comfort us. She just went in and told the principal that she had to come to see about her friend. And after we moved to Buffalo, which is about 80 miles from Rochester, when she got word that Solomon had passed, before I knew it she was at our door and she stayed with us that day and even overnight to be sure we were as best as we could be under the circumstances. Karen thanks for being a friend.

When the boys were told that they would have a difficult time holding a job, God sent people into our lives who would give them a chance to work. The Rochester Police Department gave Paul his first job as one of the teens on patrol. I was the president of the Rochester Finger Lakes Chapter for Sickle Cell and one of the board members, the Chief of Police, arranged that job for Paul. Then later, he worked at McDonald's, Burger King, and Pizza Hut. He worked while going to high school and then through college, too. Thank you all for giving my sons a place to work. That helped them as they muddled through these difficult times.

The principal at the school I worked for, Dr. Ray called me into his office one day. He knew of Paul's musical abilities and the music department in our school needed to hire a musical accompanist. With all the issues Paul had, Mr. Ray asked me if I thought Paul could handle the job. I told him that if he gave him the chance, he would do his best. Doc called Paul in for an interview and gave him the job. Paul did his best not to let him down. He'd come to work even when he was sick. There were times I'd see him walking down the hall of the school; and I knew he was in so much pain. He could hardly put one foot in front of the other. But he came to work anyway. The students loved Mr. Harris. Doc, thanks for giving Paul a chance. You know how much it meant to him, our whole family, and to me.

My sister-in law, Doris, would call the boys just to say hey and see how they were doing. When Paul got his driver's license, she gave him her car. She found out that when Paul ministered at different churches that he didn't always have a ride to get there and back home. She remembered how her brother, Vernal, had to do that down south when he first started preaching at the age of nine or ten. She didn't want Paul to have to do that, so she gave him his first car, her Lincoln Town Car. He was so proud, and, oh boy, were his friends impressed. Of course, Paul would give them all a ride, even those who didn't do the same for him. That didn't matter to him; if someone needed a ride and he could help, he did.

When Solomon was so very sick, she bought him a recliner chair so that he could rest more comfortably. That meant so much to Solomon, because this was at the time when he was nearing the end of his life. Sitting up in a comfortable chair eased his suffering some, so he could rest. Thanks Dor-Ruth-A-Bell. Your brother has taken the chair for himself now, and I know that pleases you.

One of the youth leaders of our church kept a close watch on them so they'd be able to attend one of our national youth events. Everyone called her Aunt Eva and she was another Godsend in my son's lives. It was because of her that they had one of the most fun times of their lives. We truly love you, Aunt Eva.

Toward the end of his life, Solomon had a number of complications that prevented him from being able to do things for himself anymore. My granddaughter Malaya's, mom, Nicole cared for people who were very ill and for those in a hospice unit. So when Solomon couldn't take care of himself anymore, she would go by his house (after working all night) to make him breakfast and help him get cleaned up and dressed for the day. I love you Nicky. I remember Solomon telling me he had written poems about her.

Nicky's mother, Rose, would sometimes go over and clean the house for Solomon. She would fuss at him for not doing what the doctors told him to do. Solomon liked that because it made him feel like she really cared about him. When she cooked her dinner, she would sometimes send or bring dinner to him; he liked Rose's cooking. Thank you, Rose. You know how much Solomon loved you, Rose.

His god-brother, Cyrel, who was more like a brother, was there for Solomon ever since elementary school. His mother, Beryl, was like a sister too, so whenever Solomon needed Cyrel, Aunt Beryl made it happen. When Cyrel moved into his own apartment and Solomon decided he wanted to try it on his own, Aunt Beryl stepped in and got the landlord of the apartment building to rent an apartment to Solomon. Solomon's apartment was over Cyrel's. That really worked out well at first. If Cyrel hadn't seen or spoken to Solomon in a few hours, he'd go up and check on him.

Once when Cyrel had not heard from Solomon, he almost broke the door in to see if he was alright. He didn't mess around when it came to his brother, Solomon. There were times when Solomon was in so much pain and we would have to bring him to the hospital, Cyrel would pick his god-brother up in his arms to carry him to the car.

My nephew Karl is one of the boys' closest cousins. He

would stay overnight at our house to be close to his cousins. He, too, is more like a brother to them. He spent countless hours visiting with them in the hospital. He has been there for Elijah after the passing of Paul and Solomon. Hang on Snoopy! Hang on!

Then, there is our godson, Clemon, who again is more like a brother to them. He stayed in our home, probably as much as his own, to spend time with his god-brothers. He, too, would spend hours in the hospital visiting them.

The guys would all meet at the hospital after school. The hospital staff had gotten to know them all by now and would try to give Paul and Solomon a private room to accommodate their visitors when possible. You see, one of the hardest parts of all this is that they didn't know if that visit would be the last. Their family and friends were all aware of the seriousness of each hospital admission.

Their god-brother, Chris, was the level-headed one of the group, and he still is. Thank you, Chris, for being a constant, positive influence in Elijah's life.

Our dear Regina, and her twin sister Jolene, are like daughters to us, and played pivotal roles in the lives of both Paul and Solomon. Well, I guess I should say in all three of my sons' lives because they still are there for Elijah, if and, when he needs them. These young ladies went out of their way many times to just put a smile on Paul's and Solomon's faces. They prayed for, and with, them. They laughed and cried with them. I thought for a time there that Regina was going to be my daughter in-law. (Wishful thinking on my part) She and Solomon kind of dated for a quick moment. She tried her best to get him to rethink his decision about not going to college. Solomon had watched how difficult it was for Paul, and thought he'd just not try at all. She kept telling him that he could do it. She told him, "If your brother can do it, so can you."

She saw so much potential in our Solomon, and just wanted him to try. I wish he had had as much faith in himself as she did, but when all was said and done, she was with him until the end, and I mean until the end. Solomon eventually had to move to Buffalo, New York where my husband and I had moved. My husband was pastoring a church there. It was in Buffalo where Solomon had to have hospice care. Just days before Solomon's passing, Regina took off from work in Rochester to come to be with her friend. Solomon told me, "Mom, I think Gina really does love me."

I told him, "Yes, she does, Solomon." She even stayed in the room overnight and slept on a sofa. Solomon was not talking much by this time. But he let us know that he knew Regina was there. He tried to talk to her at times. *Dear Lord thank you so much for bringing her into our lives for even such a time as time! Lord you are so amazing!*

Before we moved Solomon to Buffalo, he had to be admitted into the hospital during a routine blood transfusion appointment. Regina had been sitting with him to keep him company and help uplift his spirit. Solomon was trying to get into the bed and he started to fall. Regina caught him and broke the fall. I, still to this day, don't know how in the world she did it. When I got to the hospital, Solomon told me what had happened. "I didn't know Regina was so strong. She is too tiny to hold me up. But she did it, Mom. She caught me and helped me get in bed. I have a new respect for her. I think she loves me too."

She said, "I do love you, Solomon." He smiled. She was Solomon's Senior Prom date. He thought they were the best looking couple at the prom. She had gotten off from work and was not feeling well that night, but she refused to disappoint Solomon.

Jolene and Regina were there yet another time for our sons. They were both in the bridal party for Paul's wedding. They had become close friends with Paul's girlfriend and soon-to-be wife. They had become two of Paul's and Solomon's close friends, as well as Paul's prayer partners. I was trying to play matchmaker with Solomon and Regina.....oops was I supposed to say that? They both lovingly tolerated my failed attempts. I still think they would have made a great couple.

Brother Robert was a Godsend of a young man. He came into our lives just when we needed him most. I'm sure he had no idea of how he would have such an awesome effect on our and Solomon's life. When Solomon was not able to walk, Brother Robert would come over and pick him up to get from the bed to the wheelchair. Now mind you, Solomon was almost six feet tall and Brother Robert is about five foot three or so. It did not matter to him how difficult it was. He would come by to make sure Solomon had eaten. Solomon loved lime Kool-Aid. Brother Robert would go out of his way to find it for him. Now, he is like a son to Vernal and me. That's love. Thank you, Brother Robert.

Paul passed November 28, 2000. I knew that that Christmas was going to be very hard to get through that year. One of the things that meant so much to me was a gift that my dear friend and co-worker, Dr. Gloria Sullivan, gave me. It was an ornament that she had made. It was a clear globe that had gold bullion in the bottom with three giraffes in it. The thing that was so special was that two of the giraffes were standing and the other was lying down. When I opened the box and saw it, I started crying. I wiped my face and went over to her office to thank her. I held the ornament in front of her. When she saw it with the one giraffe lying down, she turned red in the face and began to tear. I thought she had made it that way intentionally, but she had not so she was saddened to see that the one had fallen over. But I thought she had laid the one over to represent my Paul who had gone to glory. We hugged each other and cried together. Thank you, my dear Gloria.

We met a wonderful lady named Sharon during the trip to Los Angeles. She was so kind to our Paul and made him and his brother feel so very special during our visit. She gave us a personal introduction to all the band members. She treated us as though she'd known us forever. You know, like we weren't strangers. Elijah was being a little shy and kind of stood off at first, but she was having no part of that and kept talking to Elijah until he warmed up. She still keeps in touch with us. I know God has great things in store for her. Thanks, Sharon. We are also grateful to the Starlight Foundation for what they did for Paul and Solomon.

Paul and Solomon were so proud of their brother, Elijah when he went to live with Carl Thomas and produced with, and for, him. When Carl's CD came out, they both wanted to go out to buy it so they could hear their baby brother's music on a professional's songs. Thanks Carl. Thank you for being one of our sons now. Thanks for being there for Elijah, too.

Some things may seem small and simple to others, but it meant the world to us. I will never forget the people who were there for me during some of the most painful and difficult times of my life.

I could go on and on telling you about the many wonderful people who God placed in my life who were instrumental in helping me along my journey. I really don't want to leave anyone out, so let me say thank you to all who have shown me and my family some amazing love. I really don't know how I would have made it without you.

Dear Jesus, I just want to thank you for bringing such wonderful people into our lives. Only You can do such truly timely things like that. You have an amazing way of showing your love to your creation. I will forever be thankful to you Lord, my Savior, my God, and my King! I will never stop giving you all the praise, the honor, and the glory. It all belongs to you. You know just when to place me on the hearts and minds of just the right people who help me through my dark days. Then you direct upon them to say a kind word or leave a card in my mailbox. Sometimes you just sent them by to put a smile on my sons' tear-dried faces. Lord, You are so awesome. Amen

Chapter Thirteen

A View Through Other Eyes

Sometimes it's helpful to know how others see and think of you. Here are views from the eyes of some of my family and friends of my (Paul) King David and King Solomon. Reading what they have to say gives me so much joy and peace. I hope it will give you an even better view of my boys. Their words showed me some things about my boys that I hadn't known.

I thank God for my cousin Paul, whom I loved very dearly! He was an inspiration to me and my family in so many ways. For someone who suffered with Sickle Cell all his life, but yet had a smile every time I saw him.

He stayed in pain every day, but I never heard him complain.

After I got married in 1987 and started my family, we traveled the highway every summer and stayed on Webster Avenue. Paul always gave up his bedroom, and it wasn't because he was made to do it; there was plenty of room for us to sleep anywhere else in the house, but Paul made his room our room every year.

Words cannot explain the love we had for Paul, deep down in our hearts. I believe that because of Paul, my son, Gary Tillman, II, is so talented in music. He looked up to Paul; Paul was his inspiration.

I remember the piano that was sitting in the family room. And every time we were there, Paul would have Gary, who was at the time about four-years-old, sit next to him as Paul showed Gary how to play different chords on the piano. But little did I know that Gary would become an organist in the church today; and not just an organist, but also a keyboardist and drummer.

I want to thank you, Paul, for all your love and inspiration. You are gone, but one thing is for sure, you are not forgotten. You will live forever in our hearts. Love you, your #1 cousin all the way from Detroit, Michigan.....**Alethea Tillman**

To this day, I can still see Paul and Solomon standing before me with wide, emotional eyes – little boys worried that I was unhappy, that someone had made me cry. I was a guest in the Harris home, trying to restart my life, pregnant, unsure of what to do next. It bothered Paul deeply to see me cry when I hung up from an emotional phone call with my husband. It was more than a small child feeling uncomfortable at seeing an adult cry – it was deeper. When I left Rochester to seek a new future for me and my daughter, Paul was old enough to know what faced him. He knew the health challenges he faced and had been brutally told by a doctor he would not live past his teens. He bore this like a soldier. He remained filled with hope and the same emotions for others that he shared as a child. I gave him my leather craft tools, thinking that he would enjoy, as I had during my rough times, the release that making art with these tools had given me. And we parted.

For years, Narseary and I did not see each other – My

job and family responsibilities took me on quite a journey. But whenever something desperate happened in either of lives, Narseary and I somehow found a way to call one another. When my own daughter was crossing that line from the life we hoped for her into a world of anger, drugs, violence, it was Narseary who took her in for a while to help her remember her roots. And so time passed. I will never forget coming home after a run one morning, the only thing on my mind was calling Narseary. We had moved to a new state and I had not given her my new contact information. I dialed and reached Narseary only to hear the pain in her voice. She was saying her final goodbye to Paul that very day. And then, a pain no one should have to face, she lost her Solomon. During my short visit to Buffalo to be with Narseary, even though she was grieving, I saw in her the same strength and concern for everyone around her that I saw in her boys. Genuine, loving, caring and understanding how we all must make the very most of our days.....**Elissa Lines**

Paul

I met Paul, Solomon and Elijah in 1992 through their mother's business, and from that point a friendship grew. Paul has left a pretty significant impression on my life. No matter how my tides roll forward on my beach, I see that on his beach, his footprints never washed away when the tide rolled back to sea. Some may ask how he was able to handle his assignment. To those who didn't know him well, you never knew the impression of the footprints remained in the sand until the tide rolled away, that was the time I became aware of how strong a foundation his life was built on, unwilling to compromise on anything less, standing on the word of our Lord and Savior, Jesus Christ, no matter his battle at that present time. God said it, and that was the end of it with Paul.

I never saw Paul complain about his sickness, and I would visit him in the hospital often. No matter how much pain he may have been in, he always spoke positively of himself and others around him, truly never allowing his faith to be shaken with the things of the world. I was not aware until his passing that Paul would journal daily of his conversations with God. I can't quote it verbatim but it would say something like: Today was a day full of pain in my body, but Lord I thank you for my life. Never having that kind of assignment, I could not get my head wrapped around how he was so courageous in his journey, and yet it made me seem so weak for the menial things I would complain about, pretty insignificant in nature.

But, there are three situations that I encountered with Paul that positively impacted my friendship with him, and ultimately my relationship with God: and I would like to take this opportunity to share them with you...

When I attended college in the late '90's, I had a friend at a neighboring college that I would study with from time to time. One day I rode out to his campus so that we could study together. I remember him receiving a phone call from his mother and the two of them having a conversation about his sister. I could tell from his end of the conversation that he was trying to comfort his mom regarding the situation with her. After he ended the call, I asked him if everything was okay and he stated he hated this time of the year. Apparently his 18-year-old sister collapsed while playing on her High School Volleyball team two years prior. She never recovered, and the cause of death was something along the lines of acute arrhythmia/heart murmur. His family has struggled to deal with the loss. I asked him if he ever sought comfort and understanding in prayer. He told me that God allowed it to happen, so he saw no point. I talked with my friend, but being a newbie in Christ, could not offer up too much of The Word at that time. I asked him if he would be open to talking to another person regarding God and his plan for our life and he said yes....I immediately called Paul who answered the phone and was more than willing to talk with my friend about God and the importance of having a relationship with him. That call lasted nearly one and a half hours; it appeared that my friend would have a break-through because, as Paul continued to minister to him, he began to cry. Paul ended the conversation with prayer. Later, I told my friend of Paul's condition. Paul never alluded to his illness, but yet his strength and foundation was able to help guide my friend back on the path to a relationship with God.

In 1999, Paul married the love of his life, Ms. Shona Dukes. Before he married her, he would always acknowledge her, how deep his love was for her, how much she meant to him. Throughout their marriage, he continued to acknowledge his love for all to see, but what was AMAZING to me was in the fall of 2000, Paul became very ill, to the point that he was hospitalized in ICU. The hospital staff would only allow two people back at a time for twenty minutes or so, and during my time in ICU with him and Shona, throughout all the pain medications the hospital had him on, and as this man slipped in and out of consciousness; when he spoke, it was always about how much he loved his wife, how beautiful she was and is. See, he never allowed his circumstances to change who he was inside. You could always count on Paul to be Paul. How wonderful and rare it is to love like that, but how incredibly special is it to be loved like that, too. There is no doubt in my mind that Paul approached his love for the Lord in that same manner. No matter what God allowed to take place in his life, Paul always acknowledge God as a merciful one and all he wanted to do was praise his name.....Wow!

The last time I saw Paul alive was on yet another visit to see him in the hospital. By this time, they had moved him out of ICU and placed him in a regular room. We knew the prognosis given by the doctors did not afford him much more time on this earth. I remember that day Paul began to receive a lot of visitors; I don't remember exactly how many, but I want to say something along the lines of eight. Before Paul would allow anyone to leave he said, "I want to have prayer." As Paul led us in prayer, he began to give everyone a prophetic word in the room. I know for me, I had never seen this done before and was awe-stricken that he began to minister to the very people who came to minister to him. Prior to praying, Paul lay in the bed with his eyes closed, not talking much, but when he began to give everyone a prophetic word in the room, he opened his eyes and looked at each and every one of us...it was as if he was transformed. A few days after, Paul went home to glory.

Later, as his family prepared for his home-going service, they picked out a picture of him that they wanted to use on the front of his program. It was a picture of Paul in a white tuxedo on his wedding day. No matter how they tried to reproduce the picture for the program, Paul had a blinding white light around him, a heavenly glow, and it later made me think back on how Paul lived his life, and made me wonder whether or not I had been entertaining an angel here on earth. I have known no other like him, and probably never will again.

Solomon

My dear sweet Sollie, I hardly know where to begin. Solomon and I are a lot alike in the sense that we both were ambitious at a young age. We both saw the big picture for life, but sometimes became stuck along the journey. I traveled the road, not knowing if it was going to take me to the place where I wanted to go, but I know that road was generally the direction I needed to be in. So I would walk the talk, all the while being intimidated inside, but never showing fear on the outside. For Solomon, he would always vocalize his ideas and speak it as though it were. It wasn't until his passing that I later learned the effect that I had upon his life. We were close friends, and as with Paul, I too, would sit at the hospital for hours with Solomon, keeping him company, talking about plans, ideas, etc. I would sometimes go up to the hospital with my assignments from class. I would talk to him about some of the things that I was learning and get his perspective on a paper I had written. I even asked him to attend some classes with me to help me think through some perspectives of the teachings. See, Solomon had a love for music, in fact all of his brothers were musically inclined, child prodigies if you will. Solomon loved to write poetry and Rap. He kept journals upon journals of his music, and in those lyrics, you learned his thoughts and feelings about life, that deep perspective that made him special, and his thoughts on his illness and people that were closest to him.

As time moved on, life took us in different directions, but when Solomon called, I would always answer. I remember receiving a call from Solomon in July 2009, he wanted to meet with me as he needed to brain storm some ideas to establish a nonprofit foundation for Sickle Cell patients. Because he was unsure how to do so, and I am a banker, I went up to the hospital one day after church to visit with him. We talked only briefly about the foundation, and more about things he still had yet to accomplish, some regrets, and what he needed to do to correct some decisions he made in the past. When I left the hospital that day, I only heard from Sollie, via text, here and there, asking me how I was doing. It was not until December, 2009 that I ran into a mutual friend and she told me Solomon's health had seemed to decline. I immediately contacted him so that I could come see him. One day on my lunch, I walked into the hospital and was standing outside the door where Solomon's team of doctors gave him some upsetting news regarding his treatment. I had to walk away to compose myself, and when I was finally able to go in his room, he said to me, "I know you heard what the doctors said, I am not ready to die, but I am not afraid to die either, because I know where I am going when I leave this body, but I am made of steel and can't be easily broken."

From that point on, I checked in on Sollie daily, especially since I knew he was getting treatments three times a week at the hospital. Two days before Christmas, I had a package for his mother and decided that I would drop it off at the hospital where Solomon was having an out-patient transfusion. When I arrived, however, I saw Solomon all alone in the room; and for the first time in seventeen years, I saw him cry. His pain was out of control, and he was unable to call for help. After getting a doctor to check on him, she recommended that because of the pain level, he check into emergency. He fought me on this, saying he did not want to be in the hospital on Christmas. I finally persuaded Sollie that if they can manage his pain now, that maybe they can get it under control in time enough for him to go home by Christmas. I swore to Sollie that I was not going to leave him in the hospital by himself. I picked him up and placed him in the wheelchair where we moved over to ER to get pain treatment for his crisis. I stayed with him until his father went to pick his mother up from Buffalo.

Christmas Eve, the doctors released him, so he was able to spend Christmas at home with his family. Shortly after the holidays, Solomon began communicating less and less, so I began traveling to Buffalo to see about my friend. I spent the night in hospice with him and did most of the talking, but I could see that in his eyes he was talking back to me, trying to tell me things that he never vocalized before. Over the next few weeks, I continued to check in on Sollie and my last visit with him, I was sitting on his bed, holding his hand, and he asked me to make him a pound cake. I had agreed to do so, but deep down I knew that would be my last time seeing him. As I left that final time, I kissed him on his cheek and whispered in his ear, "You are made of steel; you are the toughest man I know." And even though he did not respond, I again could see in his eyes that he understood perfectly what I said to him, and a few days after, Solomon went home to glory.

Solomon had stated that he did not want people who never gave him the time of day while he was living to be crying over him in death; that is why Sollie choose to be cremated.; He did not want to leave a permanent marker in which people could mourn him; he did not desire that because he did not die, but merely transformed. I knew that while others were crying in sadness, my tears were of rejoice because he was prepared for this journey and he was looking down on us smiling; smiling at those who knew and understood him best, and laughing at those who pretended to be the friends they never were.

If I could say anything to Solomon right now, it would be that I love you too; friendships like the one we had are hard to find. I don't care what it looked like to other people, it was never any of their business anyway!

To Paul and Solomon, thank you for being a true friend, thank you for your wisdom, and thank you for your courage...Love and miss you both...until we meet again.... **Regina**

It's hard to know where to start. Paul and Solomon Harris were two wonderful and gifted young men whom I was so proud to have been an aunt to. I was aunt, babysitter, confidant, all rolled into one (shaking my head and smiling). I still see them as little boys, and as grown men, as well.

I remember Paul playing the drums as a very small boy with anything he could get his hands on. I still see them as little boys, and as grown men, as well. If he could get some sounds out of it, it would work for him. Paul was very talented with his hands, music-wise and with art.

His drawings and paintings were just awesome!!! The day Paul played the drums as a child with the Arsenio Hall Band made him so happy and made the family so happy for him because it was a dream-come-true for him.

When Paul King David Harris graduated high school, I cried so hard because it was said he wouldn't live to see that day come. The day Paul King David Harris married, I cried even more because I never saw him happier!

The thing that I admire so much about my nephew, Paul, is that he loved GOD so much. Through all the pain and all the suffering, he held on to the Lord and nothing could shake his faith.

Paul had a very positive attitude and he shared it with others; and all the other boys looked up to him because he was the one that was the most in control. The other boys used to always love it when Paul let his silly side out. There is just so much I could say, but I can't put it all into words.

I will move on to Solomon. Solomon Harris and Paul were very different brothers, both very talented with very different personalities. Solomon was a very silly child always laughing, talking, and clowning around. Solomon loved snakes. That's why I called him Snake Man. Solomon was producing music and rapping and was very good at it. He was always a determined person.

When he set his mind on something, it was look out world!

Solomon was a GREAT father who loved his children. Till the end, he was going to start a business with me because only his Aunt Peanut would do. Sadly, that would never happen.

They will never be forgotten and will live forever because they left their imprints on this earth..... Aunt Peanut (Wanda Williams)

A true ANGEL sent by God!!! The one thing of MANY that I LOVED about Paul was his LOVING way of telling you to get it together!!! He was quiet, but yet so POWERFUL!!! No condemnation, but love and grace....he was a TRUE BROTHER and FRIEND!!! He will forever be missed!!!..............Serena Young

Paul had a way of making everyone he met feel important, so as a result there are so many professional musicians, singers, directors, praise team leaders, and ministers in our area, all because of my cousin, Minister Paul Harris, who actually lived the Word of God. ....Ken

I would go to the piano and strike any random, isolated key. Then I'd say, "Hey Paul, what note is this?"

And without hesitation, he'd always give the correct answer. "Aaah that's E-flat, two octaves above middle-C," he'd utter; followed by a little grin like the "Cheshire Cat". You see, my cousin had a gift that his peers both admired and envied: the gift of "Perfect Pitch." During my college years, my professors would encourage the students to develop their listening skills to approach that ability. But, the best we could attain was "Relative Pitch." We might get close, and periodically we'd hit the nail on the head when given a tonal center or other references. But Paul got it right all of the time--without practice, effort or any supporting variables. He just had that rare gift!

I am reminded of another Paul from the Bible. And like my cousin Paul, with his gift of perfection, this Apostle Paul was also given a measure of imperfection. Three times, we are told that this Apostle asked the Lord to take away his imperfection. And the Lord responded, "My grace is sufficient." I believe that a weight of imperfection has to balance the weight of perfection. That is the gravity that keeps us grounded here in this imperfect world. One day, God took away the imperfections from both Paul and Solomon, and their souls ascended from this imperfect world into a place of perfection.

Many years ago, I wrote a song just three days before my mother-in-law's funeral. The song is entitled "Live On (Ode to Ethel)." I dedicated the song to her and sang it at her home-going. Years later, I decided to record it, and co-produced it with my cousin Paul. After he completed the music programming and his instrumental solo, I took the tracks to my studio to add the vocals and other finishing touches. But, by the time I had mixed everything together, Paul had relocated to that ultimate music studio on Celestial Boulevard. Who knew that he would hear the final production of that song at his own home-going?

A musical genius and a gift from above is how I describe my cousin. I think about him from time to time. And when that happens, I still go over the piano and hit any random note. Then I look up and say, "Hey Paul, what note is this?"............... Brandon Vil Saint Paris

In the spring of 1995, I met the Harris family; Rev. Harris, Evangelist Narseary and their three boys Paul, Solomon, and Elijah. Narseary worked part-time as a nail technician in conjunction with her full time job as a counselor at James Madison Junior High School in Rochester, New York. Narseary was referred to me by a mutual friend; I made an appointment to have my nails done days before my High School Ball. I was a senior in high school, anxiously awaiting graduation and college.

At my first appointment, Narseary, "Mommy Seary," and I made an instantaneous connection. She had such a sweet spirit; we'd sit, drink coffee, and talk for hours. I enjoyed talking to her; the topic didn't really matter. It was just an opportunity to see her, relax, and enjoy the conversation. From the first time we met, I could see that Narseary had a pure heart and an unconditional love for God that radiated from every pore of her soul. My friendship with Paul, Solomon--"Solly," and Elijah soon flourished; on weekends I went over to their house just to "hang-out", talk to Narseary, and talk to the boys.

As time passed on, there were times I would come to visit only to find out that either Paul and/or Solomon were in the hospital. Sickle Cell is such a devastating disease, prior to meeting Paul and Solly I didn't understand the true devastation. I was friends with a young lady years prior who had passed away as a result of complications with Sickle Cell, but I did not understand the devastation--Indescribable pain, the inability to walk, sleep, and eat, etc. The list goes on and on. The pain from the cells "sickling" is absolutely horrendous. The worst part is the pain medication only "eases" the pain; the pain never completely goes away. Paul and

Solly's crises were indescribable and horrifying to watch.

I have so many memories of Paul, the most memorable moment occurred at the church where Reverend Harris and Narseary pastored in Rochester, New York, "Trinity Temple." Paul was outside with a few of his friends after service, and his friend was having car trouble; the car wouldn't start. In desperation, his friend was ready to call a tow truck but Paul said, "No tow truck is needed, just let me know when you're ready to go."

His friend replied, "So what are you going to do? You're no mechanic."

With great confidence, Paul said, "Just let me know when you're ready to go, I've got this."

Out of curiosity his friend said, "I'm ready to go."

Paul raised one hand toward Heaven and placed the other hand on the hood of the car and said, "IN THE NAME OF JESUS!" His friend turned the ignition and the car started. This is the confidence that Paul had in God.

I last saw Solly in December of 2009. Solly had just finished his treatment at Strong Memorial Hospital in Rochester, New York. When I walked into the hospital, Solly was sitting in the lobby in a wheelchair. He was swollen; his skin had turned a few shades darker. At first glance, I didn't recognize him until I heard him say in that deep Solly voice, "Hey Jolene." My heart dropped to see him sicker than I ever had before, but I smiled, held back the tears, and gave him the biggest hug I could. As we sat in the lobby talking and laughing, I realized that there was no need to be sad. Solly had lived much longer than the doctors had projected. He was growing tired and weary from his illness. From Solly's condition, at that point, I knew it would not be long before he would be gone. In the midst of all of his pain, and the illness that had taken over his body, Solly held no malice toward anyone. Solly knew at that point that he wouldn't be on earth much longer. In spite of it all, he still said, "Everything is alright between me and God."

In steadfast prayer, my sister Regina, and I watched Narseary, a loving mother; a mother who loved her children with every ounce of her being, bury two of her sons. Paul and Solly were not only God's gift to the Harris family, they were God's gift to all of the people that they knew.

The incredible strength that Narseary displayed at the loss of two of her sons is strength that can only come from above. She showed supernatural strength that only comes from God. Narseary continues to love the Lord and lift up holy hands to in praise. This is a measure of strength that only comes with true belief, faith, and confidence in God. The Lord took Paul and Solly, but we know that was a part of God's incredible plan for their lives.

The first time we met, little did I know, they would change my life forever......**Jolene**

Paul and Solomon, thanks for making me a part of this.

Paul and Solomon Harris were my godbrothers. My fondest memories of them both are when we were small children. I can remember us like it was yesterday, running around their house and sometimes mine, playing without a care in the world. In October of 1993, I decided to get married. When I asked Paul to be in my wedding, he was just as excited to be a part of the wedding as I was to have my little godbrother stand with me on my special day. Here's a funny story about how great a time Paul had at my wedding reception. Now mind you, Paul was at least 18 years old at the time. As I entertained the guests at my reception, one of my cousins came over to me and whispered in my ear that Paul seemed to be a little tipsy. Naturally, my reaction was "Who gave my godbrother some wine?"

I walked over to Paul and asked him if he was okay. Paul said, "Hey sis," with a great big smile on his face. All I could do was laugh. He was so cute and he was really enjoying himself. Knowing him, he probably had two sips of wine and that was all it took. For a long while, I had no knowledge of the grave conditions that surrounds the Sickle Cell Disease. Yet, both of my godbrothers lived with this disease and neither one of them would complain. Oh, how I miss them. I will be eternally grateful for all of the wonderful memories I have of my two loving godbrothers, Paul and Solomon Harris.....
Rasheena Green-Hoffman

Paul:

I remember so well the day that Paul King David entered my world. He was the most beautiful baby in the nursery at St. Mary's Hospital! He was the only African -American in the nursery at the time, but he looked as white as all the other babies, so the other visitors kept asking us which baby was ours. That was funny! As Paul grew older his pigmentation came in, and so did Sickle Cell Disease.

As happy as I was about his birth, I was that much and much more, saddened about this disease that we all knew very little about. As I learned more about the disease, I prayed and prayed that God would deliver my precious Paul from it.

I spent many days with Paul as he grew from a baby to one of the strongest men I have ever known; even until this day! I loved him so much!

One of my favorite memories of Paul is his graduation day from the School of The Arts. The doctors had not expected him to live to see that day, so you can imagine the pride that I felt to see my Paul walk across that stage. It was such an accomplishment because he had missed many days out of school because of his illness, but he persevered, to not only graduate, but to graduation on time! This is strength that he had demonstrated time after time that I'm talking about.

His wedding day!! Oh what great joy that day brought to all of the family from near and far; we came from Georgia, Detroit, Connecticut, Maryland, and other states and cities. And, of course right in our home town of Rochester, New York. We celebrated that day not only with Paul (and Shona), but for him. This was a day that we weren't sure if he would live to see himself, but God made it happen. I remember praying and praying that he would not be sick that day. I'm sure that I was not the only one praying that prayer. Paul was so, so happy. I can still see him in his white tuxedo waiting proudly and lovingly at the altar for his bride. That was a good day for him.

I remember the first sermon that Paul gave. Paul stuttered at times, but when he gave his sermon, there was not one stutter. He stood tall and strong at the pulpit and poured out his soul to the congregation. He spoke clearly and poignantly. I remember him being spent when he ended sermon, but still standing tall and strong.

There are so many good memories I have of my beloved Paul, of happy times in his life. I thank God for those memories because they help me get through the memories that make me cry. Memories like the times that we spent in the hospital crying and praying to God that he take this disease away from Paul. I don't know why he wasn't healed, but I know that he dealt with the disease with strength that could have only come from God. Paul never complained, even when he was enduring the worst kind of pain. He praised and loved God through it all.

I remember leaving my two children at home while I went to the hospital to sit with Paul...just to be there with him. Sometimes, I'd just sit there while he rested. Sometimes he didn't want to sleep because he thought I'd leave while he was asleep, but I assured him that I would be there when he awakened and would not leave while he was asleep. Other times we talked or watched TV together. We'd talk about his music. The other thing that Paul loved was music, actually the arts; writing, visual arts, performing arts and music. Paul loved all of the arts—visual art, the performing arts, writing, and music. I remember that my Paul was a genius and he was so, so talented in every form or art. He was truly a gifted man, and he himself, a gift from God.

I try not to think of those times too often because they remind me of too much pain and make me cry. But, those times are also a part of Paul. I try to think mostly of the good days, the days of family picnics, of family holidays; which Paul loved! Paul's best memories were of times when the family was together.

Even when Paul was leaving us, he was so concerned about family, especially his wife, Shona. I was in his hospital room in intensive care, and he told me that he was worried about Shona, and wanted us to pay more attention to her. (I never told Shona of this conversation.) I remember telling Paul that, yes we were concerned about Shona too, but that our main concern was for him. That's the kind of love that Paul had for his family.

I remember Paul's last day with us. He wanted his mom and his wife in the room with him. They were on each side of him and he said, "Now we're all together."

Yes, I remember Paul King David Harris, and will never forget him!

Solomon (Solly):

When I think of King Solomon D. Harris, I think of that old Frank Sinatra song, "I Did it My Way." Solomon was a very strong-willed person. If you said he couldn't do something, he would try with all of his might to show you that he could. Solly endured so much pain, as did his brother, Paul. But most of the time, you wouldn't know that he was in pain. Whenever you asked him how he was doing, he would answer, "All right," even when he was suffering through pain that would have sent you and me to the hospital.

When we knew that Solly was coming, we all had such hope that he would not have the dreaded Sickle Cell Disease. We couldn't conceive of such a thing. But, you know that he was diagnosed with the disease too. I asked God, *Oh, my God!! How could you allow such a thing?*

But, Solly had the disease. But, I remember happy times with him too. I remember him liking music so much, and dancing every time he heard lively music. It always brought him to his feet. I think Solomon had the first real "Happy Feet." When he heard music, no matter what he was doing, he would stop to dance.

As Solly got older, he liked to write poetry. He would write about his life, he wrote about death and having no fear of it. He wrote about his pain. When he shared his writings with me, it brought me to tears because there was such pain and strength in his words. I remember trying not to let him see me cry because I wanted to be as strong as he was. Wow!! What strength he had.

One of the things that made Solly happy, which in turn made me happy, was my visits with him when he was hospitalized. He said to me one time, "Aunt Jacquie, I like it when you and Uncle Hameed come to visit me because you stay with me. You don't come and stay for ten or fifteen minutes. You stay with me as long as I need you here."

I would do the same with him as I did with Paul. I'd say "It's okay for you to go to sleep. I'll be here when you wake up."

A memorable day for me with Solomon was the birth of his son, Solomon, Jr. I was there when his son was born. He was so proud. That was one of the happiest days in his life. I remember the love that Solomon had for his children. He wanted nothing but the very best for them as most fathers do.

When Solomon was nearing the end of his life, I spent a lot of time in Buffalo with him. The one thing that Solly looked forward to was my weekend visits to Buffalo. I made those visits, not only for Solomon, but also for Narseary and Vernal. It gave them a short time of respite. They knew that if I were there, they could just rest in the house or take some needed time away. They knew that Solomon would be taken care of in their absence.

As I was saying, Solomon would look forward to my weekly weekend visits because he LOVED his Aunt Jacquie's pancakes! I put so much love into those pancakes that he felt it!! It made no difference who was in the house; I had to be the one who made the pancakes for him. And, let me tell you that it was a pleasure and an honor to do it.

My Solomon also loved my candied yams; and whenever

he asked me to make them for him, he knew he could count on me to do it, I don't know what it was about those yams, but I do know that they made him happy, and that made me happy!

I remember one weekend; I had to work, so I told Narseary that I wouldn't be coming to Buffalo. She told me that Solomon wouldn't be happy about that. I told her to let him know that I'd be there the following weekend. Well, let me tell you...When I got off work that Saturday evening, I had to go to Buffalo, because Solomon had Narseary call me to tell me that he expected me to be there. You know I went! I could not let him down.

One night when Solomon was getting very close to the end of his days with us, I slept in his room with him in a lazy chair. When Solomon woke up that morning, he said, "Aunt Jacquie, did you sleep here all night?"

I said, "Yes, I did."

He said, "You must love me."

I said, "I love you so much!" My heart was broken and filled with love at the same time! Broken, because I knew my Solly was leaving us; and filled with love because I knew that Solomon knew that he was loved; not only by me but by his whole family. This is one of my most precious memories.

Another of my dearest memories of Solomon involves his brother, Elijah. Elijah and I were standing and talking in the kitchen of their home in Buffalo. Elijah told me that he didn't want to be there when his brother left us. I remember telling him that if that should happen, that it would be a memory that he would hold dear. As

God would have it, on February 8, 2010, after Narseary and Vernal left the hospice for a rest at home, Elijah was alone with Solomon when he left us. I asked Elijah how he felt about that. He told me he was glad he was there because he didn't want Solomon to leave with no one there; and that that he would hold that moment close.

Paul and Solomon:

I remember their home-going services. What services! For both of them, the churches were filled to capacity with family and friends. There were dignitaries from churches, from the Mayor's Office, from the City Council Office. And, as with Paul's wedding day, people came from all over. If you didn't know who the services were for, you would have thought they were for some well-known famous person. This was the caliber of their characters! They loved and were loved in return!.........
Aunt Jacqueline Williams Morgan

Chapter Fourteen

What Is Sickle Cell Anemia?

Sickle Cell Anemia is a very ugly disease. It mostly affects the African-Americans in our country, although it is not limited to only that particular race. There are still way too many children being born with this ugly disease. There are too many babies and their families suffering. Why can't someone in the field of medical research find a cure? I've been told that there is a cure in Africa. Why isn't it allowed to be brought here to the States? Why? I know people from Africa who say that people there with Sickle Cell Anemia don't suffer nearly as much as the people here do because they chew on sticks from a tree that has healing properties in them—and maybe even a cure. Why can't we get it here? I've been told also that politics prevent the help from reaching the African-American Sickle Cell Population. I believe that the chewing stick works because a friend gave us some once. For a whole year, while the boys chewed on it, they did not get nearly as sick as they had been without it. When we ran out, we tried to get more, but were unable to. Soon after we ran out of the chewing sticks, they began to have very severe crises again. As a mother watching and feeling helpless, my own pain was indescribable

It really makes me angry to believe that our government can prevent a form of relief, or even a cure, for the thousands of Americans who suffer from his horrid disease. Sickle Cell Anemia is a blood disease that came as a result of the body fighting against malaria. Many years ago in Africa there were the epidemic levels of malaria, so the body built an immunity to fight the disease. This was a good thing because the blood cell took on the shape of a sickle and the malaria was not able to live in the blood stream of people who had the sickle cell trait. The problem occurred when a child was born of both parents having the sickle cell trait. That child then had Sickle Cell Anemia. These cells would block the blood vessels in the body causing excruciating pain, swelling of the joints, blood clots, and deterioration of vital organs.

People with this disease tire easily and are limited to activities that require strenuous exercise like swimming, bike riding, running, tennis, football, baseball, wrestling --all the kinds of thing little boys like to do. It affects the kidneys and bladder causing bed wetting in some children well into their teen years. It causes slower maturity and so some children enter puberty a lot later than their peers. Some children have to have their spleens and gall bladders removed at a young age. The blood cells can also block vessels in the legs and cause ulcers to form. When these areas become infected, amputations may be necessary. Some Sicklers have strokes before they are even five years of age. There are cases of blindness and hearing loss. These are among just a few of the effects of the disease. There are many others that I have not mentioned. The list is pretty gruesome.

I recently saw on the internet that there is a cure for Sickle Cell but the cost is more than most families can afford. It is though stem cell treatment. This is another one of those bittersweet announcements.

I was so happy to hear that there is a cure, but sad-dened that it came too late for my sons and that the cost is out of reach for the ones who are still suffering. I can't imagine how horrible it must be to know that a cure is available—but only for those who can afford it. Yet this is true for so many people.

We live in a world where there so much technology and people have so much knowledge and wisdom and still there are so many unanswered questions as it relates to cure for diseases in our country.

Below is some information that describes in it more detail. Sometimes what you don't know can, not only hurt you, but it can even kill you.

Sickle Cell Disease

What is Sickle Cell Disease?

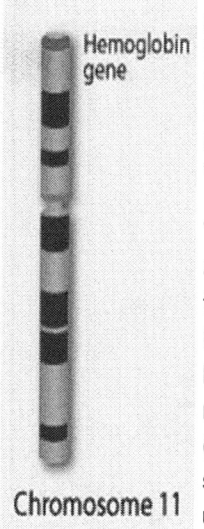

Hemoglobin gene

Chromosome 11

Sickle cell disease is a disorder that affects the red blood cells, which use a protein called hemoglobin to transport oxygen from the lungs to the rest of the body. Normally, red blood cells are round and flexible so they can travel freely through the narrow blood vessels.

The hemoglobin molecule has two parts: an alpha and a beta. Patients with sickle cell disease have a muta-tion in a gene on chromosome 11 that codes for the beta subunit of the hemoglobin protein. As a result, hemoglobin molecules don't form properly, causing red blood cells to be rigid and have a concave shape (like a sickle used to cut wheat). These irregularly shaped cells get stuck in the blood vessels and are unable to transport oxygen effectively, causing pain and damage to the organs.

How do people get sickle cell disease?

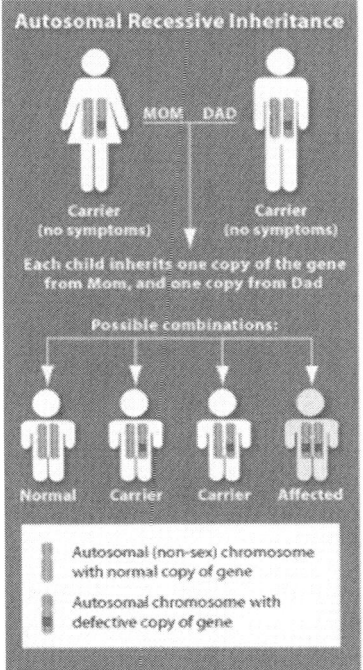

Sickle cell disease is inherited in an autosomal recessive pattern. This means that a child will not inherit the disease unless both parents pass down a defective copy of the gene. People who inherit one good copy of the gene and one mutated copy are carriers. They are clinically normal, but can still pass the defective gene to their children.

Normal hemoglobin

Sickle Cell hemoglobin forms long, inflexible chains

Normal Red Blood Cells

Sickled Red Blood Cells

Normal red blood cells are compact and flexible, enabling them to squeeze through small capillaries

Sickled red blood cells are stiff and angular, causing them to become stuck in small capillaries

What are the symptoms of sickle cell disease?

Sickle cell disease prevents oxygen from reaching the spleen, liver, kidneys, lungs, heart, or other organs, causing a lot of damage. Without oxygen, the cells that make up these organs will begin to die. For example, the spleen is often destroyed in these patients resulting in some loss of immune function. As a result, these patients often experience frequent infections.

The red blood cells of patients with sickle cell disease don't live as long as healthy red blood cells. As a result, people with this disorder often have low red blood cell counts (anemia), which is why this disease is commonly referred to as sickle cell anemia.

When sickle-shaped red blood cells get stuck in blood vessels this can cause episodes of pain called crises. Other symptoms include: delayed growth, strokes, and jaundice (yellowish hue to the skin and eyes because of liver damage).

Because of these complications, people with this disorder are likely to have their life span reduced by about 30 years.

How do doctors diagnose sickle cell disease?

Most states routinely screen newborns for sickle cell disease with a simple blood test.

If the disorder is not detected at birth, a blood sample can be used in a test called hemoglobin electrophoresis. This test will determine whether a person has sickle cell disease, or whether he or she is a carrier of the faulty hemoglobin gene.

How is sickle cell disease treated?

Babies and young children with sickle cell disease must take a daily dose of penicillin to prevent potentially deadly infections. Patients also take folic acid, which helps build new red blood cells.

Doctors advise people with sickle cell disease to get plenty of rest, drink lots of water, and avoid too much physical activity.

Blood transfusions that provide a patient with healthy red blood cells are a common treatment.

People with more severe cases of the disease can be treated with a bone marrow transplant. This procedure provides the patient with healthy red blood cells from a donor, ideally from a sibling.

Interesting facts about sickle cell disease

Unlike normal red blood cells, which can live for 120 days, sickle-shaped cells live only 10 to 20 days.

In the United States, the disease most commonly affects African-Americans. About 1 out of every 500 African-American babies born in the United States has sickle cell anemia.

Sickle cell disease is most common among people from Africa, India, the Caribbean, the Middle East, and the Mediterranean. The high prevalence of the defective gene in these regions may be due to the fact that carriers of a mutation in the beta-subunit of hemoglobin are more resistant to malaria. Malaria is a disease caused by a parasite that is transmitted to a person when they are bitten by an infected mosquito. The sometimes fatal disease is common in hot countries, and causes recurring chills and fever.

Where can I go for more information on sickle cell disease?

Sickle Cell Society

The Sickle Cell Information Center

It is my prayer that this book has and will continue to be a blessing to you and your loved ones.

May the peace of God be with you always; and know that He is in control of everything that affects our lives. Let's not focus on the problem but let's focus on the problem solver.

About the Author

Evangelist, Narseary Harris, is the wife of Elder Vernal Lee Harris, Jr. who is the pastor of the Prince of Peace Temple Church of God in Christ in the city of Buffalo, New York.

She works closely with her husband in ministry as the president of the Women's Department in the church.

She has been blessed by God to be a mother and grand-mother.

She worked for the Rochester City School District for over 25 yrs.

She is a national workshop presenter and conference keynote speaker.

She has brought the word of God in churches across New York State and several other states.

She is the Hulda Club President in New York Western First Jurisdiction COGIC and is on the executive staff of State Supervisor of Women, Mother Helena Akins under the direction of the jurisdictional Prelate Bishop Dr. James R. Wright, Sr.

She is very active in her community and serves on several committees:

The Community Engagement Committee for The New York Western Affiliate for Susan G. Komen

Chair of FLOW (First Ladies of Western New York), overseen by "The Witness Project"

American Heart Association Buffalo NY.

Chair of the Unity Conference which is now in its third year, hosted by the Prince of Peace Temple COGIC Women's Department.

She believes the people of God should strive for Spiritual Excellence and be proactive in attaining spiritual, physical, emotional, mental, and financial heath and wholeness in order to be better servants to better advance the Kingdom.

Her heart's desire is to please God in all that she says and does.